CITIZEN INVOLVEMENT IN LAND USE GOVERNANCE
Issues and Methods
by

Nelson M. Rosenbaum

THE URBAN INSTITUTE is a nonprofit research organization established in 1968 to study problems of the nation's urban communities. Independent and nonpartisan, the Institute responds to current needs for disinterested analyses and basic information and attempts to facilitate the application of this knowledge. As a part of this effort, it cooperates with federal agencies, states, cities, associations of public officials, and other organizations committed to the public interest.

The Institute's research findings and a broad range of interpretive viewpoints are published as an educational service. The research and studies forming the basis for this publication were supported by grants from The Ford Foundation and The National Science Foundation. The work was undertaken in The Urban Institute's Land Use Center.

The interpretations or conclusions in this report are those of the author and should not be attributed to The Urban Institute, its trustees, The Ford Foundation, The National Science Foundation, nor other organizations that supported this research.

CONTENTS

FIGURES

FOREWORD

During the past decade, the processes and premises of governmental control over land use have changed dramatically. The states have reassumed significant amounts of the authority previously delegated to local governments. The traditional health and safety rationale for governmental control of private land development has been broadened to include a wide range of social and environmental concerns. Planning has been accorded a more central role in guiding the exercise of regulatory authority. Citizen involvement in land use decision making has been authorized and implemented at all levels of government.

All these reforms have aroused some degree of criticism, but none has generated as much controversy as the attempt to increase citizen involvement in land use governance. Even a cursory review of recent literature reveals a wide gap between expectations and reality in the implementation of legislative mandates for citizen involvement.

Many citizen groups and concerned individuals express dissatisfaction with "token" efforts to expand their participation rights and opportunities. Legislators and elected officials in many jurisdictions criticize both the cost and the clumsiness of citizen involvement efforts. Staff planners and administrators responsible for implementing citizen involvement mandates chafe at restraints on funding and manpower that limit their ability to develop "meaningful" programs. Developers resent the delay and procedural obstacles imposed by citizen involvement requirements.

The objectives of citizen involvement and the major issues of organizational structure have not been carefully considered by legislators, elected executives, and citizen leaders in most jurisdictions. Legislative mandates often derive more from conformity to current political fashion than from a well-conceived commitment to a particular idea of democratic participation. Clearly, there is a need for more explicit consideration and more precise specification of the objectives and structure of citizen involvement programs.

This study by Nelson Rosenbaum is intended to help narrow the gap between expectations and reality. The analysis provides a framework for stimulating and guiding policy debate on the most important issues of citizen involvement in land use decision making. The author initially examines the theoretical background to the current emphasis on citizen involvement. The thrust of his argument is that direct involvement in decision making is a necessary aspect of contemporary democratic practice, representing an appropriate response to the growth in governmental authority and bureaucratic discretion. Based on this analysis, the author recommends a set of basic organizational principles which can be utilized to develop an integrated, coherent citizen involvement program.

The core of the study is a review of several major program design issues that political leaders and citizens should address in adapting basic organizational principles to particular circumstances and jurisdictions. The author provides no optimal approach to citizen involvement, no "cookbook" solution to the difficult choices among policy options. Rather, in line with the basic goal of The Urban Institute's Land Use Series, the purpose of the analysis is to contribute to more informed and reasoned debate on the issues among legislators, citizens, and elected officials—whatever the outcome of the debate may be.

The study continues with an examination of techniques and methods for implementing a citizen involvement program, and concludes with an analysis of the overall costs and benefits of citizen involvement in governmental decision making.

This is one of a continuing series of reports on current issues in land use, other titles of which are listed on the inside of the back cover. The series has been prepared under the direction of Worth Bateman in the Land Use Center of The Urban Institute.

William Gorham
President
The Urban Institute

November 1976

viii

ACKNOWLEDGMENTS

The author is indebted to Worth Bateman, Director of the Land Use Center, whose early interest in the problems of citizen involvement provided much of the stimulus for this study. Terry Sopher, NSF program manager in the Division of Advanced Environmental Research, has been a continuing source of advice and assistance. Prue Larroca provided research assistance for the project, and Mona-Marie Stockham served capably as project secretary and typist. Walt Rybeck of The Urban Institute Publications Office made important editorial suggestions on an earlier draft. Outside reviewers who contributed valuable critiques include Mike McManus, Sherry Arnstein, and Erwin Hargrove. Finally, thanks are due to members of the User's Advisory Committee, who guided the project in directions that would be most useful to state, regional, and local governments.

I. INTRODUCTION

CITIZEN INVOLVEMENT AND DEMOCRATIC PRACTICE

American democracy was founded on principles of limited governmental authority and formal public accountability. These principles, so deeply embedded in American political culture, also furnish the intellectual roots of the contemporary movement for greater citizen involvement in governmental decision making.

The demand for expanded citizen involvement represents the latest chapter in the continuing evolution of popular control over government in the United States. For more than two centuries, the fundamental objectives of democratic practice have remained constant: to insure that public policies correspond closely with the needs and preferences of affected citizens, and to prevent government from overstepping the bounds of its limited authority.

Responsiveness to citizen desires and respect for citizen rights constitute the essential underpinnings of consensual democracy. If public policy consistently diverges from the direction of public preferences or if government persistently impinges upon basic rights and liberties, the motivation for voluntary allegiance and compliance is eroded. Coercion must then be substituted for volition and the democratic system degenerates into authoritarian rule.

The historical background and philosophical significance of contemporary demands for citizen involvement in governmental decision making often have been ignored or forgotten. Citizen involvement is addressed, both in the literature and in practice, on a cynical, expedient, and self-serving level. Given the lack of positive legislative direction, bureaucrats and administrators often define citizen involvement objectives in terms of their *own* priorities and functions; these may include such goals as "enlarging public support for the agency," "mobilizing a constituency to implement the plan," or "improving the efficiency of information gathering."

None of these goals is necessarily an undesirable consequence of citizen involvement, but they are all secondary. Such objectives fail to acknowledge and respect the primary purpose of citizen participation—increasing the responsiveness and accountability of government to the citizens affected by public decisions.

The central premise of this study is that legislators and elected executives must accept active responsibility for upholding and defending the historic traditions of American democratic practice in the contemporary era. Bureaucratic and administrative power has grown

1

alarmingly in both its reach and the scope of its discretion. The expansion of opportunities for direct citizen involvement is a necessary antidote, an appropriate adaptation of democratic practice to modern conditions.

This challenge requires more than the routine inclusion of mandates for "widespread," "effective," or "meaningful" citizen involvement in statutes and ordinances. As Congress belatedly recognized in its experience with the citizen involvement provisions of the Community Action and Model Cities Programs, decisions on basic and sensitive issues of program authority and responsibility cannot be left to planners and administrators. Rather, it is essential that legislators and elected executives show a more critical and sustained interest in the objectives and organizational structure of citizen involvement programs. Officials can achieve that aim by defining more specific statutory mandates and by exercising more intensive oversight of implementation efforts.

The principal purpose of this study is to provide legislators, elected executives, and concerned citizens with the conceptual background they need to take a more active role in the design and supervision of citizen involvement programs. This goal is accomplished through analysis of (1) the historical origins of citizen involvement; (2) the basic structure of citizen involvement programs; (3) the major program design issues; and (4) the methods and techniques for implementing a citizen involvement program.

The substantive focus of the study is land use decision making—a particularly sensitive area of public policy that is at the heart of current concerns about the expansion of governmental authority. The peculiar sensitivity of land use governance and the rationale for this study are detailed below.

THE SENSITIVITY OF LAND USE GOVERNANCE

Since the beginning of the postwar movement to bring governmental decision making under greater popular control, land use planning and regulation have been high on the agenda of reform. Indeed, the first federal program to incorporate a specific mandate for citizen involvement—the urban renewal program—dealt with land use planning. The reason is that land use decisions are extraordinarily sensitive, both in the scope and immediacy of their impact.

Perhaps of foremost importance, land use decisions directly affect the enjoyment of private property rights. The drafting of a comprehensive plan, approval of a zoning variance, or review of a subdivision plat usually involves thousands and often millions of dollars in increased or decreased property values. The sensitivity of these private economic effects is, of course, explicitly recognized in the American legal tradition, which requires compensation for extreme diminution of value under the "takings clause" of the federal and state constitutions.

Over the past thirty years, the scope of private economic impacts deriving from land use decisions has increased markedly because of the dramatic rise in homeownership rates. With such a great proportion of citizens' capital assets invested in the value of residential property, public sensitivity to broad governmental authority over the land market has understandably increased.

Second, land use decisions are sensitive because they influence many other aspects of a community's lifestyle—e.g., population composition, environmental quality, recreational opportunity, and fiscal stability. In the past ten to fifteen years, these community impacts have begun to receive as much attention as private economic impacts. This attention reflects two developments. First, there has been a marked upsurge in community commitment and organization in inner-city neighborhoods, stemming largely from federal programs of the 1950s and 1960s. Second, there has been a more recent shift in the mood of suburban communities—away from accepting unfettered entrepreneurialism and rapid development, toward concern about the costs of growth and the need to preserve open space as a vital community resource. As a result, land use decisions now generate wider controversy than would derive from private economic impacts alone.

The extreme sensitivity of land use governance has resulted in numerous instances of conflict and confrontation between citizens and government. Abetted by dramatic increases in the education and income levels of the American population and by extensive political experience gained in previous social movements, citizens display extraordinary levels of mobilization and organization on land use issues. Citizen groups have demonstrated again and again that, if not satisifed with decisions, they can impede, obstruct, and delay the execution of policy for extended periods of time

This is not to justify or defend the tactics of all citizen groups. Governmental decision makers should not be intimidated by the prospect of citizen opposition and cannot attempt to appease all groups that have the potential to obstruct and delay. However, in an area involving both great sensitivity and a strong potential for public mobilization, it is pragmatic as well as theoretically desirable to maximize popular access and involvement, in the hope that delay and obstruction can be kept to a minimum.

3

Over the last five years, as the extent of governmental control over land use has dramatically expanded, the sensitivity of policy making has been increasingly recognized. Thus, citizen involvement mandates figure prominently in many legislative enactments.

At the federal level, the Coastal Zone Management Act of 1972 declares that it is national policy "to encourage the participation of the public" in the planning and execution of coastal land use management. Among recent state statutes, Oregon's well-known land use law (S.B. 100, 1973) calls for "widespread citizen involvement in all phases of the planning process." Florida's Growth Management Act (S.B. 53, 1975) requires that each city and county preparing a comprehensive plan "shall establish procedures for providing effective public participation in the comprehensive planning process."

On the county level, the official resolution establishing a new Planning and Land Use System (PLUS) in Fairfax County, Virginia, declares that officials must "assure citizen input into every phase throughout the program." The resolution also requires that citizen input "be highly integrated with the decision-making processes of the County Board."

Despite such provisions, most legislators and elected executives will admit that they have few firm ideas about what the mandates mean, and are ill prepared to supervise staff actions. Thus, planners and administrators are left with almost complete discretion to implement citizen involvement mandates as they see fit—subject only to the often crude budgetary constraints imposed by legislative action.

For these reasons—the particular sensitivity of land use decisions, the prominence of legislative mandates for citizen involvement, the ambiguity and indecision surrounding efforts to implement broad mandates—this study focuses on land use governance. It is hoped that the analysis will help improve citizen involvement programs in this field, and will also assist legislators and elected officials concerned with other areas of policy making.

II. ORIGINS AND OBJECTIVES OF CITIZEN INVOLVEMENT

The struggle for greater popular control over government in the United States is characterized by two complementary themes.

First, reform groups have traditionally devoted major efforts to expanding the scope and significance of voting participation in the American political system. The main effort has focused upon the extension of voting rights to new segments of the population, thus expanding the opportunity of those groups to gain recognition of their needs and preferences. A parallel effort has been devoted to making greater numbers of government officials subject to elections.

The second theme is the effort to supplement voting rights with opportunities for direct citizen intervention and influence in decision-making processes. The United States enjoys a more deep-rooted tradition of direct citizen involvement in government than most other democracies (e.g., the New England town meeting model), but only in the twentieth century has this tradition risen to prominence in other settings and areas. Election of governmental officials, after all, provides only an indirect and imprecise means for affecting policy. As government has grown larger and more complex, and broader discretion has been accorded to nonelected officials and administrators, the expansion of opportunities for direct intervention has become a major reform objective.

The following discussion will briefly examine the evolution of democratic practice in voting participation and will then explore in greater detail the movement for direct citizen involvement in decision-making processes.

ROLE OF VOTING PARTICIPATION

Borrowing heavily from Montesquieu, the federal constitution of 1789 and the initial state constitutions of the Revolutionary era relied primarily on the balancing of powers among the three branches of government to protect against arbitrary or capricious action by any particular official or institution. The concept of democracy embodied in the founding documents certainly did not envision the enforcement of responsiveness through accountability of public officials to a mass electorate.

The constitutions of the thirteen original states all incorporated either a property-holding or tax-paying qualification for exercise of

5

the franchise. In addition, only a few offices were subject to popular election: president and member of congress on the federal level, representative on the state level, council member on the local level. Indeed, the extent to which popular control over government was limited in the Revolutionary era may be gauged from the fact that, with the exception of the Massachusetts constitution of 1789, none of the early state constitutions was submitted to the enfranchised voters for ratification.

The movement for change in this highly restricted conception of democratic practice began almost immediately after the founding of the nation. In the period between the 1790s and the 1830s, the first great struggle for increased popular control was waged by citizen activists who hoped to extend the suffrage to all white males. The impetus for change came primarily from frontiersmen, nonlanded farmers, and the growing numbers of urban laborers and artisans who were effectively disenfranchised and politically powerless under the early constitutional acts.

The concept of broader and more intensive popular control over government first found favor, as might be expected, in the "frontier" states of Vermont, Kentucky, and New Hampshire. However, there followed a long and difficult struggle to extend the practice to the rest of the nation. In large, dominant states such as New York and Virginia, white male suffrage was bitterly resisted by established land-owning elites. Following the aristocratic conceptions of parliamentary democracy found in the writings of Locke and Burke, the landowners found the prospect of accounting to the "vulgar masses" unsettling. Nevertheless, by the 1830s, most states had adopted universal white male suffrage.

In successive periods of American political development, extending to the contemporary era, the franchise has been gradually extended to other major groups and segments of the population, including women, blacks, and youth. Each advance, accepted today as an incontrovertible aspect of normal democratic politics, was vigorously resisted by established political elites of earlier periods as a radical and dangerous innovation. Opposition was based on many of the same arguments heard in today's debates over direct citizen involvement in decision making: extending participation rights would be too costly or disruptive to government efficiency and stability; the disenfranchised group is too ignorant, uninterested, and unreliable to be entrusted with participation rights; government must be insulated from the passions of the mob.

In each case, an overriding positive principle triumphed: that government exists to serve all the people and must therefore take cognizance of their varying needs and preferences. Our basic historical impulse has been to take the risks and bear the costs associated with a broad-based, egalitarian conception of democracy.

Paralleling the struggle for liberalizing voting rights, reformers also attempted to extend the impact of the vote. During the mid-1800s a number of states first authorized direct popular election of mayors and other local administrative officials. In the same period, many state officials—including the governors, lieutenant governors, attorneys general, and some administrative officials—were also subjected to electoral tests.

This "long ballot" movement, which lay at the heart of the Jacksonian conception of democracy, was based on many of the same themes and propositions that animate the citizen involvement movement today—the desire to insure a representative bureaucracy, the mistrust of discretion exercised by an established and entrenched governing class, the emphasis on political accountability.

By the early 1900s, ballots reached extraordinary lengths as every official from water commissioner to dogcatcher was included in local elections. On the state level, most of the new regulatory commissions of the 1880s and 1890s (e.g., railroad and public utility commissions) were made elective. After a long struggle, U.S. senators were finally subjected to popular vote.

As ballot length grew, a certain amount of disillusionment set in with sole reliance on the vote as a means of popular control over government. This disillusionment was crucial in the overall evolution of American democratic practice, since it gradually deflected much interest and attention away from voting participation toward more direct mechanisms of citizen intervention and influence in decision making.

Proponents of the "short ballot" and advocates of "direct democracy" raised a number of arguments against sole reliance on the vote: (1) Most voters were unable to assemble adequate information to make intelligent choices on long lists of governmental officials; (2) Municipal- and state-level political machines exploited the long ballot by sweeping in slates of incompetent wardheelers; (3) The proliferation of elected officials made it difficult to coordinate governmental policy and to focus responsibility for success or failure; and, (4) Perhaps most importantly, the periodic election of government officials provided only a very uncertain and infrequent mode of enforcing limits upon governmental discretion.

These arguments continue to have much force today. Certainly, the vote remains the basic, most powerful technique of popular control over government. Reformers continue to struggle over extension

7

of the franchise and the appropriate scope of elections. However, there is widespread recognition that the vote alone cannot "finetune" the operation of our democracy. Important policy issues are too numerous and complex to be dealt with meaningfully in election campaigns, elections are too infrequent to have a substantial impact in enforcing responsiveness and accountability, and too much authority has been delegated to administrative officials and bureaucrats. Thus, the preeminence of the vote in American democratic practice has been increasingly challenged during the twentieth century by rediscovery of the neglected tradition of direct public involvement in decision making. The challenge has been to adapt this tradition to modern conditions and needs.

EVOLUTION OF CITIZEN INVOLVEMENT

The initial focus of the movement for direct citizen involvement in governmental decision making was expanding popular control over legislative action. This is understandable, since legislatures still dominated governmental decision making in the early 1900s.

The movement for direct citizen involvement arose primarily as a result of discontent with the arrogant and corrupt actions of state and city legislators. Given the iron grip of big-city machines on traditional partisan elections, reformers searched for some other means of insuring responsiveness to popular needs and desires and preventing arbitrary and capricious governmental actions. The approach progressives and populists of the early 1900s supported was a combination of closely related procedural innovations: initiative, referendum, and recall.

Initiative allows citizens to propose legislation by petition. Referendum provides veto power over particularly sensitive and important legislative acts. Following the tradition of innovation in democratic practice by frontier areas, South Dakota was the first state to authorize statutory initiatives and referenda in 1898, and San Francisco was the first municipality to provide for statutory referenda. From 1900 to 1920, the years of greatest "progressive" influence, twenty additional states, most in the west and midwest, adopted the initiative and referendum in some form. Initiative and referendum also spread rapidly on the municipal level under constitutional enabling provisions in thirty-three states.

The recall provides an opportunity for citizens to specify a particular set of grievances against a legislator or other elected official and to require a special election by petition. In 1903, Los Angeles was the first municipality to adopt the recall; in 1908, Oregon was the first state. In subsequent years, the recall was authorized for removal of state-level officials by fourteen states; the process was authorized at the municipal level through state enabling legislation in thirty-nine states.

During the period from 1900 to 1930, when the movement for direct involvement was focused on initiative, referendum, and recall, there was not yet much concern about popular control over the authority exercised by administrative officials—i.e., staff members of bureaucratic agencies, citizen members of regulatory commissions, appointed officials of government departments. Historically, the amount of authority allocated to appointed officials and administrators was small. As Lord Bryce noted about the American version of democracy during the 1880s,

It is a great merit of American government that it relies very little on officials (i.e. administrators) and arms them with little power of arbitrary interference. The reader who has followed the description of Federal authorities, state authorities, county and city or township authorities, may think there is a great deal of administration; but the reason why their descriptions are necessarily so minute is because the powers of each authority are so carefully and closely restricted.[1]

Expansion of Administrative Power

The beginnings of change in this pattern of strong legislatures and weak bureaucracies are found in the early 1900s. As part of the overall "progressive" effort to contain the power of corrupt legislatures, reformers fought to insulate the bureaucracy from gross political pressure through the introduction of professional civil service systems based on the merit principle. Efforts also were made to strengthen the independence of citizen regulatory commissions, such as the Interstate Commerce Commission on the federal level and public utility commissions on the state level. On the local level, reformers emphasized new forms of organization such as the council-manager system, which broadened administrative prerogatives.

The center of progressive influence in expanding administrative autonomy and discretion—both within its own agencies and commissions and, by example and encouragement, at state and local levels—was the federal government.

---

1. James Bryce, *The American Commonwealth* (1888), quoted in Theodore Lowi, *The End of Liberalism* (New York: W. W. Norton & Company, 1969), pp. 128–129.

In the early 1920s, to take a crucial example, the Commerce Department, under Secretary Herbert Hoover, prepared, publicized, and prosyletized the Standard State Zoning Enabling Act and Standard City Planning Enabling Act. Upon enactment by state legislatures, these laws allowed local governments to set up planning and zoning commissions. These independent bodies, in conjunction with their professional administrative staffs, were vested with extremely wide discretion (e.g., "promoting the health, safety, morals, or the general welfare of the community"), and their decisions were subject only to often cursory review by local legislative bodies and potential appeal to the courts.

The pressure of abrupt economic collapse in the 1930s resulted in a rapid acceleration of this trend toward expansion of administrative power. Many specialized administrative bureaucracies and new regulatory agencies were established and provided with extremely broad discretionary powers. As James Landis noted in his classic essay, the delegation of broad powers to agencies resulted from a profound feeling of helplessness on the part of the traditional branches of government: "The administrative process is, in essence, our generation's answer to the inadequacy of the judicial and legislative processes."[2]

The new federal programs of the 1930s and 1940s also spawned large bureaucracies at the state and local levels, particularly in the social services. The reliance of these bureaucracies on federal funding provided an extra layer of insulation from "parochial" political pressure and control.

During this period of enormous expansion of discretionary authority in administrative agencies, there was still great faith that the "neutral competence" and "professionalism" of the newly expanded bureaucracies and commissions would lead to accurate, rational determination of the broad public interest and to efficient management of the government. Of course, there were some vocal opponents of the departure from carefully specified mandates and limited authority, but these critics came primarily from the ranks of the "vested interests" whose actions were subject to governmental regulation and scrutiny. Since most of the protest came from those whose activity was deemed to be contrary to the broad "public interest," the criticism merely reinforced confidence in the objectivity and respon-

2. James Landis, *The Administrative Process* (New Haven: Yale University Press, 1938), p. 46.

siveness of administrative agencies. Only a few prescient independent observers in law and political science perceived the great danger to democratic practice in the delegation of such broad discretion to administrative bureaucracies and independent commissions.[3]

It was not until after World War II that public concern about the control of administrative discretion began to develop into a major force. This concern was stimulated by a number of factors, including pervasive discontent with oppressive wartime administrative controls and growing unhappiness among minority and low-income groups over arbitrary and arrogant bureaucratic decision making in the development of new social programs.

Perhaps the single most important factor in the genesis of the movement to bring the bureaucracies under greater public control was the recognition that the aggressive, adversary relationship between regulatory agencies and regulated parties that prevailed during the New Deal era had been transformed into a more comfortable cooperative posture. As numerous critics and observers discovered, regulators and regulated parties formed powerful, autonomous "subgovernments," within which bargaining and backscratching were the prevailing norms.[4]

This cooptation or "capture" of the bureaucracies and commissions, particularly at the federal level, was widespread enough to cause severe disillusionment with the doctrines of "neutral competence" and "professional objectivity." This disillusionment led to a return of the traditional emphasis on strong popular control over government.

Approaches to Popular Control

Over the last thirty years, two broad schools of thought have competed on the issue of how administrative decision making can best be brought under firm popular guidance and control. One school emphasizes the need to assert popular control through the

---

3. See, for example, A. Wolfe, "Will and Reason in Economic Life," 1 *Journal of Social Philosophy* 218 (1936); R. Cushman, *The Independent Regulatory Commissions* (New York: Oxford University Press, 1941); Herman Finer, "Administrative Responsibility in Democratic Government," 1 *Public Administration Review* 335 (1941).

4. Major early examples of the "subgovernment" literature are Marver Bernstein, *Regulating Business by Independent Commission* (Princeton: Princeton University Press, 1955), and Samuel P. Huntington, "The Marasmus of the ICC: The Commission, The Railroads and the Public Interest," *Yale Law Journal* (1952). For a similar indictment of land use regulatory agencies, see Richard Babcock, *The Zoning Game* (Madison, Wis.: University of Wisconsin Press, 1966).

elected branches of government, with the public playing an *indirect* role through the vote. The other school of thought, which is of immediate interest in this study, stresses the need for *direct* citizen intervention in administrative action.

Within the first school of thought, most observers have focused their criticism on the legislatures for their failure to specify precise standards and rules in legislative mandates to administrative agencies.[5] The delegation of broad discretionary policy-making authority, it is charged, stems more from laziness, habit, and political cowardice than from necessity. In this view, legislatures should also exercise vigorous and continuous oversight over the actions of administrative agencies, thereby stimulating responsiveness and enforcing accountability.

These arguments have had some impact on legislative behavior. On the federal level, for example, Congress has established specific standards for the guidance of administrative decision making in the areas of air and water quality control. Such standards were unheard of in previous regulatory statutes. During the past decade, there has also been a dramatic upsurge in the amount of oversight activity in Congress.

State and local legislatures have also been more vigorous in guiding the exercise of administrative discretion. In the area of land use, for example, the Florida Environmental Land and Water Management Act of 1972 was severely criticized as establishing a "process without a policy"—i.e., conferring an enormous amount of administrative discretion on a planning and regulatory agency without any substantive guidance and controls. The Florida legislature responded to this criticism in two ways: first, by establishing in 1973 a special oversight process for the review and approval of growth management rules; and second, by enacting in 1974 a statement of growth management goals for the guidance of administrative agencies. A similar legislative contraction of administrative discretion took place during 1975 in Hawaii when the legislature adopted a set of land use goals and guidelines to bring the previously unfettered State Land Use Commission under stronger popular control.

---

5. One of the most prominent contemporary advocates of strict legislative standards is Theodore Lowi. See Lowi, *End of Liberalism,* pp. 287–312. See also Henry Friendly, *The Federal Administrative Agencies* (Cambridge, Mass.: Harvard University Press, 1962), pp. 163–175. This school of thought derives, of course, from the older legal tradition of concern about improper delegation of legislative power. See E. Freund, *Administrative Powers Over Persons and Property* (Chicago: University of Chicago Press, 1928).

These examples are, however, relatively isolated. Even with the benefit of enormous staff resources, the legislative norm in Congress remains the broad delegation of discretionary authority. Oversight is spotty, depending on the personal interest and ideology of the relevant committee chairperson. At state and local levels, the ability of legislatures to supervise administrative action is limited further by the part-time character of legislative work. Thus, while some legislatures have demonstrated that they can exercise close supervision of administrative action, the promise of active control remains largely unfulfilled.

A second theme in this school of thought is the effort to increase the capacity for coordination and control of administrative agencies by elected executives. Many critics and observers maintain that chief executives must concentrate power in their offices so as to bend the bureaucracy to the will of the people, as expressed in their electoral mandate.[6] This doctrine of strong executive leadership has been embraced by many presidents, governors, and mayors in the postwar era.

In many cases, governments have been reorganized with this doctrine in mind, but the results have not been highly encouraging in terms of reasserting popular control. First, there is an inherent danger of excessive concentration of authority and abuse of discretion by the chief executive—a problem especially apparent at the federal level. Second, this approach places extraordinary and unrealistic burdens on the electoral process as a means of conveying public opinion on a wide range of activities and agencies. Given the typical nature of election campaigns for top executive offices, it is rare that sufficient information is exchanged to fulfill these functions. Finally, the ability of strong executive leaders to control administrative discretion and insure responsiveness to public preferences is limited by such personal factors as lack of time, lack of interest, and poor legislative-executive relations.

As an alternative to increased legislative and/or executive direction over administrative decision making, the reemerging tradition of direct citizen involvement in government has made itself felt with great force in the postwar era. The major impetus for expansion of

---

6. Major works in this tradition include Richard Neustadt, *Presidential Leadership* (New York: John Wiley & Sons, 1950); Charles Hyneman, *Bureaucracy in a Democracy* (New York: Harper, 1950); Paul Appleby, *Policy and Administration* (University, Ala.: University of Alabama Press, 1949); Roscoe C. Martin, ed., *Public Administration and Democracy* (Syracuse, N.Y.: Syracuse University Press, 1965).

direct participation rights and opportunities has come from three groups.[7]

First, many social scientists and policy analysts have stressed the need for direct public involvement because of disillusionment with the ability of legislatures and executives to improve responsiveness and accountability. These advocates have also emphasized that direct participation in decision making is valuable in itself as a means of building a sense of responsibility and self-confidence on the part of alienated and disadvantaged members of society.

Second, the direct involvement approach has been pushed strongly by many traditional middle-class supporters of "good government"—e.g., neighborhood associations, environmental organizations, and consumer groups. From the perspective of these citizens, direct participation is valued as a means of counteracting and overcoming the privileged relationship between administrative agencies and the vested interests they are supposed to regulate.

Finally, direct citizen involvement has been emphasized and supported by blacks, poor people, youth, and other disadvantaged groups who view participation rights as a means of obtaining more responsiveness from social service and community development bureaucracies.

Legislative and executive response to advocacy of direct citizen involvement in administrative decision making has taken two courses: (1) passage of *general procedural acts and ordinances* facilitating access and accountability, and (2) inclusion of legislative mandates in statutes and ordinances requiring administrative agencies to establish *systematic citizen involvement programs.*

Establishment of Participation Rights

The landmark Federal Administrative Procedure Act of 1946 was the opening round in the expansion of the general participation rights and opportunities of the public.[8] By requiring agencies to meet

---

7. On the background of demands for direct citizen involvement in government, see Carl Stenberg, "Citizens and the Administrative State: From Participation to Power," 32 *Public Administration Review* 190 (1972); John Strange, "The Impact of Citizen Participation Upon Public Administration," 32 *Public Administration Review* 457 (1972); Herbert Kaufman, "Administrative Decentralization and Political Power," 29 *Public Administration Review* 3 (1969); and Alan Altshuler, *Community Control* (New York: Pegasus, 1970).

8. On the general evolution of public participation rights in administrative law, originating in the Administrative Procedure Act of 1946, see K. Davis, *Administrative Law Treatise* (St. Paul, Minn.: West, 1958); E. Gellhorn, "Public Participation in Administrative Proceedings," 81 *Yale Law Journal* 359 (1972); and Richard Stewart, "The Reformation of American Administrative Law," 88 *Harvard Law Review* 1669 (1975).

certain minimum standards of fairness and openness in their decision-making procedures, and by vesting citizens with the right to judicial relief in case of agency failure to comply, the Administrative Procedure Act broke new ground in enforcing public access and bureaucratic accountability. Minimal involvement opportunities, such as mandatory public hearings or review and comment on proposed regulations in the *Federal Register,* were first authorized by the Administrative Procedure Act and its subsequent amendments. Following the normal process of diffusion and emulation, most states and localities adopted administrative procedure acts of their own during the 1950s and 1960s.

In the 1960s, as federal programs again expanded rapidly and several new popular movements developed (e.g., civil rights, consumer, and environmental movements), attention again turned to the expansion and protection of general public participation rights in administrative decision making. The most significant acts on the federal level were the Freedom of Information Act (1966) and the National Environmental Policy Act (1970), both of which created broad new information and accountability obligations for administrative agencies and made these rights judicially enforceable by the individual citizen. In the past few years, these acts have also spread rapidly at the state level and, to a lesser degree, at the local level.

The states have also pioneered in the expansion of general participation rights and opportunities. Most prominently, it is at the state level that "sunshine laws" or open-meeting acts originated. Most states now have laws requiring all meetings of administrative agencies to be open to public attendance. Even more significantly, some states have pioneered in codifying explicit sets of participation standards to which all administrative agencies must adhere. For example, Montana's 1972 constitution requires citizen participation in the operations of all government agencies, and a recent statute in that state provides a comprehensive set of procedural minimums with which agencies must comply.

While general acts and orders of the type discussed above establish a framework of accessibility and accountability that is the necessary core of citizen involvement in administrative decision making, they are not sufficient to insure that an agency will become more responsive to popular preferences. In the timeless ways of the bureaucracy, minima have a tendency to become maxima. Open meetings, notification procedures, public hearings, and other formal rights in and of themselves do not necessarily produce greater popular guidance and control. These procedural norms are passive; they may or may not be used positively to bring about a change in decision-making patterns. Recognizing these limitations, many groups have demanded more specific legislative mandates for citizen involvement which place an affirmative obligation on administrative agencies to solicit participation in particular policy decisions.

Authorization of Systematic Involvement Programs

The Federal Housing Act of 1954 was the first major statute to incorporate a specific mandate for citizen participation. After five years of contentious and frustrating experience with federally financed urban redevelopment under the Housing Act of 1949, the revised statute sought to make administrative decision making more responsive to popular needs and desires by requiring a *program* of citizen participation in the planning and execution of projects. The new concept was incorporated in the statute as a response to critics who claimed that the urban redevelopment had resulted in a brutal, inhumane approach to social problems.[9]

As in the area of general participation rights, congressional attention to the need for specific citizen involvement programs accelerated greatly in the 1960s, as vast new social programs were authorized and citizen discontent and militance increased. The well-known mandate for "maximum feasible participation of the residents of the area and members of the group served" was incorporated in the Community Action Program legislation of 1964 as a significant expression of this concern. The desire to keep administrative descretion under control was also evident in the mandate for "widespread participation" of affected citizens in the planning and execution of the Model Cities program (1966).

Because of the prominence of the Community Action and Model Cities programs in the arsenal of Great Society efforts to aid urban areas, the experiences with citizen participation under these mandates have been subjected to an enormous amount of publicity and analysis over the last decade.[10] Despite the critical nature of much of this commentary, it was these two federal statutes, more than any other sources, that popularized and legitimized the concept of sys-

---

9. James Q. Wilson, "Planning and Politics: Citizen Participation in Urban Renewal," 29 *Journal of the American Institute of Planners,* 242 (1963); J. Clarence Davies III, *Neighborhood Groups and Urban Renewal* (New York: Columbia University Press, 1965).

10. The voluminous commentary on citizen participation in the Community Action and Model Cities programs is reviewed, cataloged, and analyzed in John Strange, "Citizen Participation in Community Action and Model Cities Programs," 32 *Public Administration Review* 655 (1972). See also "Symposium on Citizen Action in Model Cities, CAP Programs," 32 *Public Administration Review* 377–470 (1972).

tematic citizen involvement programs, a concept subsequently incorporated in many other pieces of legislation at all levels of government. Indeed, the need for positive programs of citizen involvement in administrative decision making seems to have become a new norm—although, as previously stressed, much confusion and uncertainty remains among legislators and elected executives about the meaning of the terms "widespread," "effective," or "meaningful" citizen involvement.

With administrative agencies increasingly required to operate under more rigorous requirements for citizen access and involvement, reform efforts have recently turned toward establishing similar opportunities for popular participation in legislative decision making. Referendum and initiative remain the most powerful and direct means of citizen intervention in legislative action, but these methods are quite clumsy and ponderous. They provide only a simple yes-no approach to public influence in the development of legislation.

Fueled by discontent with the political corruption of some legislators and distrust of the lobbying power exercised by specialized interest groups, several changes in legislative practice have been implemented in the past few years. One of the most prominent reforms promoting access and accountability is the application of open-meeting requirements to legislative deliberations. This reform is most common at the state level, but Congress currently is implementing legislative openness requirements and many local legislatures also operate under such self-imposed rules. The crucial function of these sunshine laws is to open the meetings of legislative committees so that citizens can be made aware of the crucial trade-offs and compromises that take place off the floor of the legislature.

Derived directly from the example of systematic citizen involvement in administrative decision making, another significant change is the authorization of major citizen-oriented study efforts designed to inform and guide legislative action on sensitive issues. The best known of such efforts are the "Goals" programs, such as Alternatives for Washington and the Commission on Minnesota's Future on the state level, or Austin Tomorrow and Goals for Carbondale on the municipal level. These programs attempt to clarify citizen priorities and preferences prior to budgetary or other basic decisions by the legislature.

SUMMARY

We are today in the midst of profound changes in American democratic practice. These changes are deeply rooted in the historic

American tradition of close popular control over government, but also represent new departures in the relationship between citizens and decision makers. Most importantly, there is no longer exclusive reliance on elections as the major means of influencing governmental decision making. Starting with the referendum and initiative in the early 1900s, reformers have increasingly emphasized the need to enforce responsiveness and accountability through direct citizen intervention and involvement in decision making (see Figure 1).

In the postwar era, from the early administrative procedure acts through the citizen-involvement mandates of the present, the focus of reform efforts has been on improving the process of administrative decision making. As bureaucracies and agencies have grown dramatically in power and size, citizens have demanded and received more rigorous safeguards of access, openness, fairness, and redress. The objectives of this reform effort are quite simple and straightforward: to insure a reasonable correspondence between public policy and public preferences, and to prevent arbitrary and capricious trans-

Figure 1

**FORMAL OPPORTUNITIES FOR CITIZEN INVOLVEMENT
IN GOVERNMENTAL DECISION MAKING**

	Indirect Involvement	*Direct Involvement*
A. Legislative decision making	Partisan or non-partisan election of legislators and chief executives	Initiative and referendum
	Recall of legislators and chief executives	"Goals" programs and citizen participation on legislative advisory committees
B. Administrative decision making	Partisan or non-partisan election of selected administrative officials	Participation opportunities under administrative procedure acts, sunshine acts, freedom of information acts, and related statutes
	Legislative and/or executive oversight of administrative decisions	Mandated citizen involvement programs

gression by government upon fundamental individual rights. The demand for increased participation rights and opportunities has also spilled over into the legislative arena, particularly in such basic and highly sensitive areas as the formulation of growth policy.

At this point in the evolution of American democracy, the new participation requirements and opportunities are achieving general acceptance as normal and necessary aspects of decision making. We have not yet learned, however, how to carry out these new aspects of democratic practice in an efficient and coherent manner. The remainder of this study is devoted to intensive analysis of one major challenge—the design and implementation of programs for systematic citizen involvement in administrative decision making, with special emphasis on land use.

III. THE STRUCTURE OF CITIZEN INVOLVEMENT PROGRAMS

The inclusion of specific citizen involvement mandates in statutes and ordinances denotes recognition by legislators and chief executives that uncoordinated, passive participation rights authorized by general procedural acts do not represent an adequate response to the problem of increasing responsiveness to public desires. But how can general participation rights and opportunities be integrated within a larger framework of citizen involvement? How can supplementary methods of involving the public be deployed in a coherent, goal-oriented manner? In short, what is a citizen involvement *program?*

This section presents a general framework for the organization of citizen involvement programs, consisting of a set of simple sequential components. The three basic components or phases of a citizen involvement program are (1) public preparation, (2) citizen participation, and (3) governmental accountability. Within each basic component there are a number of tasks or subcomponents (see Figure 2), each of which performs a necessary function in attaining the overall democratic objectives of increasing fairness and responsiveness.

This framework of components is not presented as a rigid hierarchical sequence, nor is it the only way of conceiving the tasks of citizen involvement. However, the model does provide a logical structure for involvement programs that can be applied usefully across all types of conditions and jurisdictions.

PUBLIC PREPARATION

The public preparation component of a citizen involvement program involves providing affected citizens with the background they need to make a constructive and informed contribution to policy making. The preparation component breaks down into two subcomponents: (1) educating the public on the basic concepts and processes of decision making; and (2) providing accurate, understandable information about current policy issues and notifying the public about opportunities to participate.

The basic education subcomponent lays the foundation for the rest of the involvement program. Affected citizens cannot absorb current policy information or express their preferences meaningfully if they do not have a grasp of what land use planning and regulation are about and how government is set up to deal with these functions.

Figure 2

STRUCTURE OF CITIZEN INVOLVEMENT PROGRAMS

Component	Tasks
A. Public preparation	Provide educational background on basic concepts and governmental organization for decision making
	Notify citizens and distribute information about current policy issues
B. Citizen participation	Work with members of the affected public to define feasible policy options
	Measure aggregate support for each policy alternative among the affected public as a whole
C. Governmental accountability	Explain the rationale of policy decisions to the affected public
	Provide means for the affected public to test the fairness and responsiveness of decisions

The primary objective of the basic education subcomponent is to improve comprehension and communication between decision makers and affected citizens. Misunderstanding between these two groups is a major source of the hostility and conflict that often pervade efforts to involve citizens in land use governance.

The entire burden of basic policy education need not rest with the administrative agency itself. This task is eminently suited to cooperation with the private sector. Schools can offer courses in land use governance, neighborhood citizen organizations can assist by disseminating their established expertise on land use matters through community meetings, the news media can be helpful in developing stories and broadcasts, and labor unions and businesses can offer educational programs at work.

The government's role in these types of activities can be limited, at relatively small cost, to providing encouragement, supervising content, and coordinating timing. Some agencies, particularly at the local level, have been quite active in stimulating such activities. Many, however, in the absence of legislative or executive requirements, have ignored the task of basic education altogether.

The second subcomponent of public preparation involves notifying citizens about current policy issues and providing useful, comprehensible information on the stakes involved in these decisions. Affected citizens cannot participate meaningfully if they are unaware that issues are coming up for decision, or if they receive only a few day's notice to prepare themselves. Again, much of the "negativism" and "irrational" opposition to land development that planners and administrators attribute to citizens may be caused by the fact that pending policy decisions are often exposed to public input only a short time before final action is scheduled.

In recent years, significant progress has been made with the passage of general procedural statutes such as freedom of information acts and sunshine laws. However, the typical procedural minimums established in such laws—such as thirty days' notice of public hearings in newspapers of record—do not address the broader need for notice to a wide spectrum of citizens who may be affected by a decision. What is required is a simple but systematic approach, such as a large-type weekly newspaper advertisement or a bulletin mailed to a large sample of households in an affected area.

Similarly, citizens cannot express themselves meaningfully if they are not provided with useful policy information. Many citizen involvement programs have been crippled by a tendency among professionals to expect citizens to understand jargon or to comprehend the highest level of technical expertise and sophistication. Thus, for example, the current information subcomponent of one citizen involvement program consisted of making detailed environmental impact statements on proposed projects available at public libraries in affected areas. This may be fine for the "quasi professionals" among the public, but it hardly assists the participation of a wide range of affected citizens. Affected citizens need pass no test of sophistication and expertise in order to claim the right to be informed and to exercise influence on public policy.

Of course, an effective citizen involvement program ultimately rests on a certain fundamental level of citizen interest, attentiveness, and understanding. Public officials cannot be expected to dramatize and oversimplify policy issues, nor can they force citizens to inform themselves. However, reasonable efforts should be made to provide current information in a variety of formats suitable for different levels of sophistication.

CITIZEN PARTICIPATION

The citizen participation component of an involvement program refers to the opportunities provided to the affected public to express preferences on proposed decisions. The citizen participation component logically divides into two subcomponents: (1) identifying feasible policy options, and (2) estimating aggregate support among the affected public for each major alternative.

Separation of these subcomponents does not necessarily mean that one must follow the other sequentially, for often one method can accomplish both tasks simultaneously. For example, public workshops may help to clarify distinctive policy positions and may also provide estimates of aggregate support for each position among those attending. However, the subcomponents are conceptually distinct and are emphasized as separate tasks to highlight the need for explicit attention to each.

The first task of citizen participation—identifying feasible policy options—involves soliciting the expression of preferences from as wide a range of affected citizens as possible. Opportunities for participation in this phase should initially be relatively unstructured, allowing citizens to define the stakes of the issue as they see them. Unstructured expressions of preference may be quite idiosyncratic, rambling, or emotional from the government official's point of view, but they serve a vital purpose in fully ventilating an issue—bringing out the full diversity of distinctive positions among the affected public.

It is the planner's and administrator's responsibility to gradually impose a structure on the public debate by highlighting the common elements among public viewpoints and by weeding out those policy options that are not feasible on technical, legal, or other grounds. Optimally, citizen participation can ultimately focus on a small number of distinctive policy alternatives that define the limits of potential popular acceptability and technical feasibility. Of course, some decision-making contexts may require the planner and administrator to impose a greater initial structure on the public debate than in other situations. But this does not invalidate the general principle that it is desirable to allow the parameters of policy debate to evolve from citizens' perceptions and preferences.

The second subcomponent of citizen participation is estimating aggregate support among the affected public for each of the basic policy positions identified. Since the central objective of citizen involvement in land use governance is to help guide the exercise of governmental authority in accordance with majority or plurality preferences, this task constitutes the crucial intelligence phase of the citizen involvement program.

GOVERNMENTAL ACCOUNTABILITY

The final component of a citizen involvement program is governmental accountability, which incorporates two subcomponents: (1) explaining the rationale for particular policy decisions, and (2) providing opportunities for formal testing of decisions that affected citizens may feel are unfair, arbitrary, or unresponsive.

Explaining the rationale of a policy decision in an explicit, comprehensive manner is a rather novel concept in American democratic practice. Public officials have traditionally expected the affected public to accept decisions without much discussion of the reasoning underlying them. In recent years, as ideological convictions and political conditions have changed, there has been an increasing demand for explicit accounting by decision makers.

Accounting for governmental decisions in a program of citizen involvement in land use governance must deal with two different aspects of citizen input. First, every individual or group that takes the time to express a policy preference in detail should receive some sort of official response, explaining what action was taken and why. This type of feedback is not only common courtesy but also a crucial means of building both public trust in the responsiveness of government and feelings of political efficacy.

Some officials may be appalled at the thought of preparing individual responses. However, a number of jurisdictions have demonstrated that such replies need not be excessively burdensome. For example, the city of Coventry, England, prepared a public "decision document" at the conclusion of its recent structure planning effort. This document responded to more than 500 individual comments by grouping similar suggestions, indicating acceptance or rejection of each, and presenting a one paragraph explanation of the rationale. It is not really technique that is at issue here, but rather the need for public officials to recognize and accept accountability obligations. These obligations must be spelled out explicitly in the language of legislative mandates.

The second aspect of feedback is explaining how estimates of aggregate preferences were used in making final decisions. The primary purpose of this task is to demonstrate that decision makers are aware of the basic direction of majority or plurality preference and have incorporated this knowledge in their deliberations. A secondary objective is to build greater support for a policy decision among affected citizens who do not personally favor the final course of action, but who might support the decision if shown that it was arrived at in a fair, sensitive, and responsive manner. A fundamental assumption of democratic government is that process is as important as policy—

i.e., that citizens will accept and support decisions arrived at fairly even if they disagree with the substance of those decisions. This proposition should be tested in a citizen involvement program.

The final subcomponent of governmental accountability involves providing opportunities for appeal and reconsideration of decisions that citizens may feel are unfair and unresponsive. In some cases, these opportunities will be provided by automatic legislative and/or executive review of administrative decisions. However, as noted in Chapter I, legislatures and executives do not always enjoy the time, interest, or capability to exercise proper scrutiny and oversight over administrative actions. Some alternative means of testing should thus be provided, such as internal review of administrative decisions by ombudsmen or citizen advocates, citizen access to the courts, or citizen-initiated referenda.

As previously noted, these types of appeal rights raise difficult and sensitive issues of balance between the appropriate prerogatives of citizens and government. Government officials cannot allow themselves to be paralyzed into inaction by endless reconsideration of decisions. This has become a very controversial issue on the federal level, for example, with regard to the use of environmental litigation under the National Environmental Policy Act to block energy-related plans and projects. On the other hand all of the education, information dissemination, participation, and accounting may fail to fulfill democratic objectives if citizens are not provided with some leverage to forestall and overturn unfair and unresponsive decisions. This balancing of prerogatives is a matter with which every legislature must grapple on its own, in the light of local conditions and customs. There is no universally applicable prescription or optimal solution.

IV. DESIGNING A CITIZEN INVOLVEMENT PROGRAM: POLICY ISSUES

Citizen involvement in land use governance takes place within many different decision-making contexts, including general goal setting, preparing rules and regulations, and applying rules to specific projects and parcels of land. Citizen involvement also takes place within many different governmental contexts—federal, regional, state, and local. Obviously, there are no universal prescriptions for the optimal design of citizen involvement programs. What is shared, however, is a common framework of necessary components and tasks (see Chapter III) and a set of basic policy issues that extends across the entire range of contexts. These issues fit into two general categories:

    1. Who should participate in land use controversies—i.e. what is the affected public?

    2. How should public involvement be organized—i.e. what units, if any, are most appropriate?

This chapter will identify the major policy problems and options within these two basic areas, and will present the arguments supporting major alternatives. The analysis is aimed at assisting legislators and chief executives to critically examine their own expectations and assumptions about citizen involvement so they may provide more substantive guidance on the design of involvement programs to administrative officials. This does not mean that legislative mandates must provide detailed guidelines on each of these issues; however, a clear indication of legislative intent should at least be available in committee reports, floor debate, and executive orders. The choices among the policy options are too important to be left to staff members of administrative agencies.

IDENTIFYING AFFECTED CITIZENS

What constitutes the affected public in land use controversies? To whom should the preparation, participation, and accountability efforts of administrative agencies be directed? These decisions constitute the most fundamental policy choices in the design of citizen involvement programs.

The basic democratic prescription is that the relevant public consists of all citizens whose life, liberty, or property will be in any way affected by governmental action. However, it is difficult both in theory and practice to specify the potential impacts of most land use decisions in a manner that precisely identifies specific classes of affected citizens. Therefore, planners and administrators typically fall back upon two simpler *prima facie* criteria of impact: (1) residence within the political boundaries of the jurisdiction in which the administrative agency operates, and (2) manifestation of voluntary interest and activity on land use issues. The question elected officials must face is whether these criteria are adequate or whether others are more appropriate.

Jurisdictional Residence

The principal arguments for using jurisdictional residence as a criterion for defining the affected public are that (1) such an approach keeps the costs of an involvement program relatively fixed, and (2) that it meshes other components of a citizen involvement program with established mechanisms of formal accountability such as referenda and recall, which are available only to residents of the jurisdiction involved. In addition, the fiscal impact of land use decisions in increasing or decreasing property taxes typically falls largely on residents of the decision-making jurisdiction.

As we are increasingly aware, however, impacts of land use decisions do not always respect established jurisdictional boundaries.[1] For example, a large suburban shopping center may stimulate traffic congestion in many surrounding communities, a major industrial complex can precipitate severe pressures for urban development in neighboring areas, or a local sewage treatment plant may affect vital recreational or scenic resources used by the residents of many neighboring jurisdictions.

In theory at least, the problem of extrajurisdictional impacts may be dealt with in several ways other than voluntary extension of the scope of a citizen involvement program. First, authority can be at least partially shifted upward to encompass a larger proportion of affected citizens within a new decision-making jurisdiction. This eliminates the policy issue of citizen involvement for the original jurisdiction. Under our system of government, however, characterized by

---

1. For an introduction to the "externalities" problem in land use control, see William K. Reilly (ed.), *The Use of Land: A Citizen's Policy Guide to Urban Growth* (New York: Thomas Y. Crowell, 1973), and Council on Environmental Quality, *Environmental Quality: The Fifth Annual Report of the Council on Environmental Quality* (Washington, D.C.: U.S. Government Printing Office, 1974).

extreme sensitivity about local home rule and state's rights, these shifts rarely take place easily or rapidly. Indeed, while recent efforts to shift certain aspects of land use authority to regional and state levels of government have achieved some success, such laws still face a very difficult political struggle in most parts of the country.[2]

As a second alternative, the interests of affected citizens outside the boundaries of the primary decision-making jurisdiction may be represented and defended through some form of intergovernmental cooperation and coordination. Over the past decade, for example, many local governments have voluntarily joined together in councils of government (COGs) through which interjurisdictional issues in transportation, land use, and other matters may be resolved.

There are two difficulties with this approach. First, the efficacy of such intergovernmental bodies in influencing the decisions of planning and administrative agencies within member jurisdictions is subject to considerable doubt. Second, the interests and preferences of particular classes of affected citizens within member jurisdictions are filtered up through a long, involved process of election and selection before being represented in such intergovernmental bodies.

The intergovernmental coordination approach is perhaps most valid and useful on the level of general planning and goal setting—i.e., when the decisions involved are broad enough and important enough that they affect a broad spectrum of citizens in many other jurisdictions. The intergovernmental approach is least useful with regard to specific cases of project approval, zoning regulation, and so forth, which affect only a small number of citizens within a few other jurisdictions.

Given the rarity of jurisdictional realignment and the limitations of intergovernmental coordination, most jurisdictions must face the question directly: Should an administrative agency take cognizance of the interests and preferences of citizens who reside outside jurisdictional boundaries if they are affected by land use decisions? The principal argument in favor of extending the reach of a citizen involvement program is respect for equity. If citizens are equally affected by a proposed action, should they not have an equal chance to influence the outcome, regardless of the accidents and political sensitivity of jurisdictional boundaries? Another basic argument for

---

2. The politics of innovation in state land use control is discussed in Nelson Rosenbaum, *Land Use and the Legislatures: The Politics of State Innovation* (Washington, D.C.: The Urban Institute, 1976).

extending participation rights is the expectation of reciprocity. It may be anticipated that the other jurisdictions whose citizens are afforded participation rights will respond in kind.

The major argument against the extension of participation rights and opportunities is that it creates indeterminacy in the cost and scope of the involvement program. At what level or magnitude of impact will an individual or group outside jurisdictional boundaries be accorded participatory status? If the criterion adopted is too broad, the time and monetary costs of citizen involvement may easily get out of hand. Jurisdictions have addressed this problem in several different ways. Perhaps the most common approach to expanding a program to citizens living outside the decision-making jurisdiction is according participatory status to those who work or own property within the jurisdiction. This narrow approach keeps the extension of citizen involvement within definable bounds. Thus, for example, the government of Dare County, N.C., made a significant effort to contact out-of-state property owners during its recent comprehensive planning process. Or in Washington, D.C., the Municipal Planning Office established a citizen's task force to plan for the Tenley Circle area which included not only residents of the neighborhood but also representatives of those who work in the area.

The other common approach to expanding the scope of citizen involvement programs beyond jurisdictional boundaries involves according participatory status to those who manifest a high level of voluntary concern. In California, for example, the Central Coast Coastal Zone Conservation Commission decided to extend its involvement program to include affected citizens from inland counties who were vocally concerned about the impact of coastal land use regulations on water quality and supply. In Vermont, the state Environmental Board and its regional commissions have granted "interested party" status to individuals and citizen groups from outside the relevant area who petition to be included in land use regulatory proceedings under Act 250.

Regardless of what criterion is selected, the extension of a citizen involvement program beyond jurisdictional boundaries represents a very difficult innovation for most legislators and executives. Elected officials are ultimately responsible, after all, to the resident voters of their jurisdiction, who may not welcome attention to the preferences of nonresidents. On the other hand, elected officials must also recognize their responsibility for the basic democratic principle that decisions should not be made by government without an opportunity for political expression. This applies with particular force to specific planning and zoning decisions in which direct economic impacts may fall on property owners living outside jurisdictional boundaries.[3] At the least, legislators and executives have an obligation to confront this issue explicity in the design of a citizen involvement program.

Interest and Activity Level

The second major aspect of identifying the affected public involves deciding whether administrative agencies should be required to seek out and involve individuals who may be affected by a decision, but who do not manifest voluntary interest and concern about the outcome. The traditional administrative approach to this issue is that a citizen involvement program should be focused on those who manifest volitional interest.

This approach rests on a strong historic background in American democratic practice. In contrast to some European democracies, United States citizens have not been strongly prodded during most of our history to participate in the conduct of political life. For example, voting registration and party membership are voluntary in the United States. Unlike many other democracies, there are no penalties for failure to vote. This tradition rests on the argument that the impacts of governmental decisions are, in the final analysis, subjective. Some individuals may be bothered by a certain level of air pollution, others may not. Some may be outraged by an increase in property taxes, others may not care. Those who are bothered and who do care will, in this view, join together with like-minded others to form voluntary interest groupings, and will seek out and use whatever opportunities are provided or can be found to influence public policy. The task of government in this interest representation approach is to seek a reasonable accommodation among the various interest groupings that make up the affected public.[4]

---

3. Under existing zoning enabling acts, abutting property owners enjoy certain mandatory participation rights such as notice and standing, regardless of where they reside. The issue, however, is which other property owners should be involved and what other types of involvement opportunities should be provided. For a discussion of these questions in relation to the American Law Institute Code, see David Hoeh, "Participation and the Proposed A.L.I. Model Land Development Code," paper presented to the 57th Annual Conference of the American Institute of Planners, San Antonio, Texas, 1975.

4. For an influential analysis of the interest-representation approach, see Avery Leiserson, *Administrative Regulation: A Study in Interest Representation* (Chicago: University of Chicago Press, 1942). The dominance of the interest representation approach in contemporary administrative practice is detailed in Grant McConnell, *Private Power and American Democracy* (New York: Random House, 1970). See also Theodore Lowi, *The End of Liberalism* (New York: W.W. Norton & Co., 1969).

The difficulty with this approach to citizen involvement lies in the assumption that all citizens enjoy equal resources for political mobilization and organization. In fact, as numerous studies have shown, political skills and resources are distributed very unevenly among the American public. Because of differences in family background, educational experience, and personality, the affluent, white, professionally employed segments of the public are much more likely than any other segments of the citizenry to organize voluntarily and intervene effectively in government. Thus, for example, in the metropolitan suburbs, where affluent white families are concentrated, extremely high levels of voluntary organization membership and political involvement are common. Here the interest representation approach seems a natural and normal choice. Indeed, the intensity of interest in land use issues is often so high that the problem becomes how to *contain* participation. In rural and inner-city contexts, on the other hand, or in large-scale jurisdictions that incorporate many different types of populations, very few individuals and interest groupings may be primed for participation in relation to the potential numbers of affected citizens.

During the last decade, the traditional assumption that citizen involvement should be focused on those who show voluntary interest and activity has been challenged vigorously. The challenge was spearheaded by the citizen involvement mandates and regulations of the Community Action and Model Cities programs, both of which placed great emphasis on stimulating and activating traditionally passive residents of poor, inner-city neighborhoods. This "outreach" approach was based primarily on the argument for equity—the belief that all individuals for whom program benefits were intended should have some say in their disposition. This basic argument was supplemented and, indeed, often overshadowed by another proposition— that once inactive, alienated, and mistrustful citizens were successfully involved in influencing decisions, the cycle of helplessness and hopelessness could be broken and voluntary levels of interest and activity could be increased.[5] Thus, beyond the need for equitable treatment, deliberate efforts to involve inactive segments of the population could fulfill the positive democratic function of political education.

---

5. See Melvin Mogulof, *Citizen Participation: A Review and Commentary on Federal Policies and Practices* (Washington, D.C.: The Urban Institute, 1970); Peter Morris and Martin Rein, *Dilemmas of Social Reform: Poverty and Community Action in the United States* (New York: Atherton Press, 1969).

Following the Model Cities and Community Action experiences, a number of statutes have incorporated the new approach, typically expressed in the call for "widespread participation" or "representation of all segments" of the affected public. However, as the results of the Community Action and Model Cities efforts remind us, some serious pitfalls are involved in such efforts. One of the principal dangers of this approach is the potential for manipulation of inactive and unsophisticated citizens by the professionals who attempt to mobilize and guide their involvement. For example, the prevalent distrust between the "advocacy planners" of the Model Cities program and the poor citizens they attempted to involve greatly frustrated that program.[6] As long as the impulse for involvement comes from *without* rather than *within*, citizens are likely to feel manipulated and professionals frustrated.

Second, evaluation of experience with citizen involvement programs attempting to solicit participation from inactive and unconcerned citizens demonstrates that such efforts are often futile. Despite massive educational and publicity efforts in many neighborhoods, turnout rates for elections to community boards under the Community Action and Model Cities programs were abysmally low. For example, community action elections rarely attracted more than 10 percent of eligible neighborhood residents on the national average.[7]

In addition, optimistic expectations about transforming behavior patterns during adulthood were found to be basically unrealistic. Despite some success in fostering new community organizations in low-income, inner-city areas, the Model Cities and Community Action programs did not generate a large number of new community leaders. Rather, they merely provided prominent vehicles for citizens who had already demonstrated a propensity for organizational involvement and leadership.

The final argument against adoption of this approach is that outreach is extraordinarily expensive, requiring special community organization personnel, special media treatment of complex subjects, in-

---

6. Lisa Peattie, "Reflections on Advocacy Planning," 34 *Journal of the American Institute of Planners* 80–88 (1968); Frances Fox Piven, "Whom Does the Advocate Planner Serve," 1 *Social Policy* 34–41 (1970).

7. See Paul Peterson, "Forms of Representation: Participation of the Poor in the Community Action Program," 64 *American Political Science Review* 491–507 (1970); Alan Altshuler, *Community Control: The Black Demand For Participation in Large American Cities* (New York: Pegasus, 1970) pp. 138–139.

tense efforts to inform citizens and other special efforts. This is not to say that the extra cost may not be necessary and justifiable, but it should be stressed that cost is a significant factor to consider in choosing among options.

In sum, choosing the correct approach to this issue presents an extremely difficult problem for legislators and executives. While the quest for representativeness in an involvement program may be costly and ultimately quixotic, the outreach approach rests on the basic social principle of insuring equity and fairness. On the other hand, the interest representation option is consistent with American democratic traditions and offers the virtues of greater efficiency and parsimony. Despite the difficulty of this decision, it is vital that elected officials confront the issue directly. Failure to do so leaves the choice in the hands of administrative personnel who are clearly inappropriate for the task.

SELECTING ORGANIZATIONAL UNITS

How can citizen involvement programs be organized systematically over large areas, substantial populations, and long time spans? This question has challenged large cities for some time and is increasing in importance as counties, regions, and states assume expanded land use responsibilities. The core issue is whether affected citizens should be approached and involved directly as a collection of individuals or whether a citizen involvement program should be organized around representational units, such as subordinate governmental jurisdictions or voluntary interest organizations.

In terms of both efficiency and comprehensiveness, the latter strategy has much appeal. On the other hand, the quality of information transmitted through intervening units may be less complete and representative of citizen preferences than a program based upon direct contact. In addition, there is always the danger of encouraging and subsidizing the local parochialism so often found in land use conflicts. In short, this is another set of difficult issues requiring explicit resolution by elected officials rather than by administrative or planning staff. The following discussion will consider two aspects of the issue separately; first, governmental units and second, private organizations.

Subordinate Jurisdictions

Should citizen involvement in land use governance be screened and mediated by units of government smaller than the decision-making jurisdiction itself? The "default" response to this question is usually negative. Most planners and administrators assume that a citizen involvement program should be built around individual participation rights and direct contact with citizens. However, in the past few years there has been increased advocacy of such an intermediary and coordinating role for subordinate governmental units, particularly in the context of newly expanded regional and state land use programs.

In Massachusetts, for example, a 1975 statute established a statewide growth policy planning process based explicitly on citizen involvement conducted through local governments. Local jurisdictions are encouraged to organize growth policy committees consisting of citizen representatives and public officials, through which the concerns and needs of local residents can be voiced to state planning officials. State growth policy will then be established by aggregating and synthesizing the contributions of the local organizing units.

This approach contrasts sharply, for example, with the approach to citizen involvement in the development of State Planning Goals and Guidelines in Oregon. In that state, the Land Conservation and Development Commission relied exclusively on direct contact with thousands of individual Oregonians through public workshops held across the state.

On the municipal level, most jurisdictions continue to rely on direct contact between citizens and decision makers, but the use of subordinate organizational units has recently increased in large cities. As part of the overall resurgence in the status of the neighborhood as a meaningful spatial and social unit, several cities have created subordinate governments in neighborhoods to act as organizing units for transmitting information and preferences between citizens and officials. For example, in Dayton, Ohio, elected Neighborhood Priority Boards are accorded a central role in reviewing and commenting upon proposed land use policies and permitting decisions. In Washington, D.C., elected Advisory Neighborhood Commissions have been established. The commissions are chartered as official agencies for the transmittal of neighborhood views to the Municipal Planning Office, Zoning Commission, and other city agencies.

The basic arguments for the use of subordinate jurisdictions are three. First, many observers and critics of government in the United States maintain that the neighborhood or, at most, the small municipality is the effective focus of the average citizen's emotional and intellectual concern about public policy.[8] It is the immediate surrounding territory and its problems that tap the most deep-seated sources of interest and involvement. Thus, it is argued, the way to involve citizens in larger planning and regulatory programs is to demonstrate their relevance to the neighborhood or municipality. This demonstration may logically be conducted through the governmental structure of the neighborhood or municipality itself.

Second, use of neighborhood governments, municipalities, or other jurisdictions as organizational units provides a comprehensive and systematic framework for an involvement program. If all units within a large area can be induced or required to participate, geographic representation can be secured without a major effort on the part of the superior jurisdiction to stimulate individual participation.

Finally, the use of subordinate units also offers the advantages of efficiency. Many of the subordinate jurisdictions will be engaged in some type of land use planning and regulation on their own. A jurisdiction of larger scale that uses subordinate units can tap these existing resources to lower its own costs. In addition, reliance on the smaller units helps to reduce "involvement fatigue." Citizens can invest just so much time in involvement, can attend just so many meetings, can respond to just so many surveys. The greater the coordination that jurisdictions can achieve in meshing their citizen involvement requirements and programs, the lesser the demands made upon the busy citizen.

Reliance on subordinate governmental jurisdictions as the organizational units of a citizen involvement program thus promises a number of advantages and benefits, both to the citizen participant and the superior jurisdiction. However, before authorizing such an approach to this vital element of program design, legislators and elected executives should carefully consider several serious pitfalls.

Perhaps the foremost problem is that reliance on subordinate jurisdictions may help to foster and perpetuate geographical and social parochialism. Official recognition of geographical distinctions as the basis of representation helps to legitimize a narrow focus on local impacts, to the exclusion of broader concerns and perspectives. Of course, there is no assurance that individual citizens will adopt a nonparochial view of land use issues either. Indeed, the experience of

8. Milton Kotler, *Neighborhood Government: The Local Foundations of Political Life* (Indianapolis: Bobbs-Merrill, 1969); Alan Altshuler, *Community Control;* Howard Hallman, *Neighborhood Government in a Metropolitan Setting* (Beverly Hills: Sage, 1974). For a contrary view, see Peter Eisinger, "Support for Urban Control Sharing at the Mass Level," 7 *American Journal of Political Science* 669–694 (1973).

most citizen involvement programs indicates that educating the public to see the broader implications of land use decisions is one of the most difficult challenges of program implementation, no matter how the program is organized. However, since reliance on subordinate governmental units is likely to increase the challenge, there are grounds for serious concern about adopting this organizational approach.

A second problem with this approach is that it tends to perpetuate the sense of distance and distrust between citizens and decision makers of higher level jurisdictions. Unfamiliarity and the distrust it breeds are major difficulties, for example, in many new state land use programs. Through extensive direct contact with citizens, officials of large-scale jurisdictions can attempt to bridge the sense of distance. Relying on subordinate units to organize and transmit the results of citizen involvement does nothing to dissolve the "we-them" attitude and may indeed reinforce it.

A final caution relates to the quality of the information about citizen preferences transmitted through subordinate governmental units. The typical posture of subordinate units is to report only the compromise or consensus position of citizen participants. Thus, the richness of input provided by contact with individual citizens is often lost. The dissenting view, the expert opinion, the personal experience may be subordinated within the overall preference pattern reported by subordinate units.

In most programs, there will still be some opportunities for direct expression of views to decision makers through letters or public hearings. But many citizens may resent feeling cut off from direct contact with the decision makers of higher level jurisdictions. Of course, from some officials' perspective, one of the *attractions* of the subordinate unit approach may be to cut down the volume of the information flow. Yet there is certainly a basis for concern about overly restricting the flow of valuable information from individual citizens.

There are both substantial advantages and disadvantages to reliance on subordinate governmental jurisdictions as organizational units in citizen involvement programs. The trade-off between design alternatives seems quite even in theory and must be determined in practice by careful consideration of local circumstances by legislators and elected executives. If subordinate units are selected, the program should incorporate some minimum standards of fairness and representativeness to which each subordinate jurisdiction must conform. Without such controls, the variability in the type and quality of information transmitted by different jurisdictions is likely to be so great as to preclude an effective citizen involvement program.

Private, Voluntary Associations

Should a citizen involvement program be organized around and accord special standing to private interest groups? Whatever the design decisions reached on jurisdictional residence, on outreach to inactive citizens, and on the use of subordinate jurisdictions, legislators and elected executives must eventually face the independent issue of exactly what role private associations will play.

A focus on established private groups is perhaps the predictable design choice. These organizations are ubiquitous and politically powerful. They typically make extravagant representational claims and loudly demand special recognition and status. However, there are also numerous reasons for caution in organizing an involvement program around such groups.

In the area of land use planning and regulation, two types of groups have been the most insistent and aggressive in demanding special organizational standing and prerogatives: first, associations of businesspeople, developers, farmers, and other large landowners who have a direct economic stake in the general pattern of land use in a community; and second, associations of residential property owners, usually organized in neighborhood civic groups or betterment organizations, who have a direct economic stake in the specific pattern of land use in their immediate vicinity.

These groups are often joined in demands for special recognition by narrower special-interest groups such as conservation and environmental associations, sportsmen's clubs, and good government organizations, based on their members' ideological, social, or recreational interests.

Jurisdictions have conferred special prerogatives and organizational standing on such private, voluntary associations in a variety of ways. One of the simplest, most common approaches is reserving a special place on advisory committees for representatives of particular groups. Another approach is providing private groups with privileged intervenor status in land use regulatory proceedings. For example, the Model Land Development Code of the American Law Institute (A.L.I.) automatically provides interested-party status in administrative hearings to neighborhood civic organizations meeting certain standards of size and representation.[9] All individual citizens, on the other

---

9. The American Law Institute, *A Model Land Development Code* (Philadelphia: American Law Institute, 1975), Sections 2–304.

hand, must convince the hearing officer that they have a "significant interest" in the subject matter before being granted official standing in the proceedings.

Some jurisdictions have gone beyond these simple procedural arrangements to accord a more systematic organizational role to private associations. In Portland, Oregon, for example, the entire land use planning and regulatory process is based on a network of private neighborhood civic organizations coordinated by the city's Office of Neighborhood Associations.[10] These organizations have primary responsibility for soliciting and transmitting citizen input on a wide variety of planning and regulatory matters. In San Diego, the city government delegates official land use planning responsibility to selected neighborhood organizations that fulfill certain criteria of open membership and structure.[11] Similarly, some jurisdictions help subsidize the production of "alternative plans" by private voluntary associations. These plans serve as principal background documents in the development of official plans and policies.

The attractions of organizing a citizen involvement program around the private, voluntary associations are clear and straightforward. First, the leaders and active members of such associations are typically highly knowledgeable and sophisticated about land use planning and regulation. Even in opposition, they are easier and more comfortable to deal with than the less articulate and interested citizens. These individuals speak the same jargon as decision makers, read the same publications and research studies, and can be relied upon to be "responsible" in presenting and defending a position.

Second, if one accepts the typical broad claims of representation at face value, reliance on such organizations provides an efficient and convenient means of consulting with large groups of concerned citizens at relatively low cost.

Third, since these groups have the greatest potential for effective obstruction and delay of decision making, there is a natural inclination to take the views of their leaders most seriously and to try to accommodate them whenever possible.

Finally, of course, the essence of the matter is that these groups exist as tangible manifestations of interest and concern about land

---

10. Mary Pedersen, "Neighborhood Organization in Portland, Oregon," unpublished manuscript, Office of Neighborhood Associations, City of Portland, 1975.

11. Douglas Harman, *Citizen Involvement in Urban Planning: The San Diego Experiment* (San Diego: Public Affairs Research Institute, San Diego College, 1968).

use matters. It is easier to accept and recognize this voluntary activity as deserving special recognition than to challenge and deny it. Without such organizations, planners and administrators would be thrown back completely on their own conceptions in identifying and consulting with the affected public. Certainly, special recognition of such voluntary organizations does not eliminate the need to consider the interests of inactive and unorganized citizens who may be affected by a decision. However, that recognition does provide a firm base from which to explore unfamiliar territory.

Despite the manifest attractions of reliance on private associations as organizational units, there has been growing skepticism and criticism recently about the dominance of such groups in citizen involvement programs. Perhaps the foremost criticism concerns the representational claims of such groups. Private, voluntary organizations are notoriously hazy about the size of their membership, attendance at meetings, percentage of active compared to passive participants, and similar matters. In addition, numerous critics and observers have questioned the extent of internal democracy within such organizations.[12] Leadership tends to be perpetuated by a small group of activists who dominate association operations. Thus, there is often a valid question about whom the leadership of these association represents.

A second problem with reliance on private, voluntary associations is that they tend to operate by consensus. Of course, the presentation of a united front is understandable since this is the way to maximize political influence. However, the presentation of consensual positions does raise serious questions about the quality of information reaching decision makers. The heart of a citizen involvement program is a free, open, and lively debate about options and alternatives. To the extent that voluntary organizations fail to report significant dissenting opinions and personal views, the richness of the debate is lost.

If a citizen involvement program is to be organized around private, voluntary associations, some effort should be made to address these problems. Perhaps the most common approach is requiring private organizations that are granted special status to conform to certain standards of open membership and procedural fairness, as in

---

12. See, for example, R. Robert Linowes and Don Allensworth, *The Politics of Land Use: Planning, Zoning and the Private Developer* (New York: Praeger, 1973).

Portland, Oregon, and San Diego, California. These efforts, however, have aroused considerable opposition from the citizen organizations, particularly the neighborhood groups, which resent intrusion upon what they consider to be their own organizational prerogatives. Despite such opposition, legislators and elected executives must insist upon establishing and enforcing appropriate standards. Special prerogatives and organizational status are privileges, not rights. The alternative of consulting directly with active and interested citizens is always available.

V. IMPLEMENTING A CITIZEN INVOLVEMENT PROGRAM: INNOVATIVE METHODS

Within the basic design of a citizen involvement program, the selection of implementation techniques and methods typically is left to the staff of the administrative agency involved. Nevertheless, it is important for legislators, elected officials, and concerned citizens to be familiar with the tools of citizen involvement so that they may effectively oversee staff actions and suggest alternatives. This section describes and illustrates briefly some of the more innovative methods of citizen involvement that go beyond the normal procedural minimums in each category.

PREPARATION METHODOLOGY

Basic Education

How can members of the affected public be provided with basic educational background on land use matters so that they may absorb current policy information and make an informed contribution to policy debate? A typical set of "minimum" procedures might include using a speaker's bureau, distributing a brief brochure to citizen groups, and soliciting background coverage from the news media.

Two types of basic educational efforts that go beyond such minimums are production of a simplified land use curriculum designed specifically for citizens, and special television programs to capture public attention and impart basic concepts. In both approaches, a number of agencies have successfully worked with private sector organizations to keep down costs.

The Princeton *Planning and Design Workbook for Community Participation* is one prominent example of a basic curriculum on land use matters for citizens.[1] The workbook, a 592-page looseleaf volume, was produced by faculty members in the Princeton University School of Architecture and Urban Planning at the request of the New Jersey Department of Community Affairs. It provides a comprehensive

---

1. Research Center for Urban and Environmental Planning, *Planning and Design Workbook for Community Participation* (Princeton, N.J.: School of Architecture and Urban Planning, Princeton University, 1969).

checklist approach to analysis of community needs and the translation of these needs into a plan. The idea for a simple step-by-step analysis of urban planning arose from experience with members of low-income citizen groups who had no idea of how to evaluate a project or a plan.

Feedback on the effectiveness of the Princeton workbook has been ambivalent. According to a survey of professional planners who attempted to use the workbook with community groups, the material is too detailed, lengthy, and jargon-laden to be of great value in working with citizens.[2] Only 12 percent of those surveyed indicated that the workbook had been used successfully with citizen groups. However, the survey did uncover a great deal of enthusiasm for the basic idea of citizens guide to processes of land use governance. Similar efforts to develop a general volume for citizen education have been undertaken by a wide range of educational institutions, including M.I.T., Lewis and Clark College, and the University of Arkansas.[3]

A similar but less detailed educational tool is the *Citizen's Handbook on Neighborhood Planning,* distributed by the city and county of Tulsa, Oklahoma, as part of its citizen involvement program.[4] In contrast to the Princeton effort, the Tulsa handbook is a brief, seventy-page paperbound volume illustrated with photographs and cartoons. It presents a general analysis of land use planning and regulation as well as a specific discussion of planning and regulatory processes in the Tulsa area. The handbook also includes a glossary of key terms so that citizens can better understand planning discussions.

Distribution of the handbook to neighborhood groups and civic associations is typically accompanied by a lecture and slide presentation. While citizen usage of the Tulsa handbook has not yet been empirically evaluated, the publication is a concise, well-organized, although somewhat pedantic, effort to present essential material on land use administration to nonprofessionals. Similar types of popular

2. Lance Brown and Dorothy Whitman, *Planning and Design Workbook for Community Participation: An Evaluation Report* (Princeton, N.J.: School of Architecture and Urban Planning, Princeton University, 1973).

3. John Platt et al., *Citizen's Handbook on Neighborhood Land Planning* (Portland, Ore.: Northwestern School of Law, Lewis and Clark College, 1973); Lajos Heder, Victor Karin, and Mark Francis, *Harvard Square Planning Workbook* (Cambridge, Mass.: M.I.T. Laboratory of Architecture and Planning, 1973); *Planning the Non-Urban Community* (Fayetteville, Ark.: City Planning Division, University of Arkansas, 1969).

4. Tulsa Metropolitan Area Planning Commission, *Citizen Handbook for Neighborhood Planning* (Tulsa, Okla.: Community Planning Associates, 1973).

handbooks are being used in Atlanta, Georgia, East Orange, New Jersey, and other jurisdictions across the country.[5]

With regard to special television programming, one effort of note is the "Choices for '76" educational campaign conducted by the Regional Plan Association (RPA) of New York, in cooperation with many jurisdictions in the area. During 1973, five one-hour documentaries on land use problems in the New York metropolitan region were broadcast over nineteen television stations in the three-state area. These documentaries were based on a book entitled *How to Save Urban America,* written by RPA staff members and distributed widely in the New York area.[6] To insure a large audience for the programs, some 6,000 "Town Meeting Groups" were organized in schools, homes, and churches. Members of these groups watched the television programs and discussed the issues together. Total viewership of the five documentaries was approximately 3 million.[7]

The "Choices for '76" campaign is particularly noteworthy in two respects. First, educational background was integrated with discussion of specific problems. This contrasts markedly with the rather vague and generalized format of many educational efforts. Second, through advertisements and direct mail, RPA distributed "issue ballots" on which citizens could designate their policy concerns and preferences after watching and discussing each documentary. Some 131,000 issue ballots were returned in response to the five programs. This balloting procedure—modeled loosely after the call-in technique used on "The Advocates" public television series—provided a positive and concrete focus for the educational campaign. However, there was some adverse reaction to the highly structured nature of the ballots.[8] The need for an appropriate ballot format should be kept in mind by any jurisdiction contemplating the use of this approach.

---

5. Atlanta Department of Planning, *How to Do Neighborhood Planning* (Atlanta, Ga.: ABC Management Consultants, 1974); *Your Voice in the Future* (East Orange, N.J.: East Orange Planning Department, 1972). See also *Citizen's Guide to the Metropolitan Council* (Minneapolis, Minn.: The Metropolitan Council, 1973); *A Citizen's Guide to Planning and Development* (Roanoke, Va.: City Planning Department, 1971); *Citizen's Guide to Planning and Zoning* (Lincoln, Ill.: Logan County Regional Planning Commission, 1974).

6. William Caldwell, ed., *How to Save Urban America* (New York: Regional Plan Association, 1973).

7. William B. Shore et al., *Listening to the Metropolis: An Evaluation of the New York Region's Choices for 76 Mass Media Town Meetings* (New York: Regional Plan Association, 1974), p. 16.

8. Ibid., p. 43.

A similar educational campaign on land use issues was sponsored by the League of Women Voters Education Fund, in cooperation with the Citizen's Advisory Committee of the Council on Environmental Quality. In the spring of 1974, more than fifty cable television stations across the nation donated an hour of air time for special land use programming, the announced purpose of which was "to heighten citizen interest and participation in setting public policy on an issue of critical public importance." Each one-hour program included a film about basic problems of land use governance across the nation, entitled "The Use of Land," as well as a presentation about specific land use issues and processes in each community (the latter prepared by local League chapters).

The value of this campaign lies in its attempt to engage public attention by linking the national perspective (stressing the scope and seriousness of land use probelms) with analysis of local concerns (presenting information on specific processes over which the citizen may have some direct influence).[9] This approach could be used in any context of overlapping jurisdictions—e.g., state-local or local-neighborhood.

Notification and Information

"Minimum" techniques used in this component typically include depositing informational materials on major community issues in local public libraries, posting public notices, and soliciting media coverage.

One technique for more systematic distribution of information to affected citizens is developing a registry of interested individuals and groups to whom detailed materials on current planning and regulatory matters in specific areas are sent. For example, the District of Columbia has developed a registry process through which the Advisory Neighborhood Commissions receive notice and current information about land use issues in their areas.[10] Such information must be sent to the neighborhood groups at least thirty days in advance to insure adequate distribution to local residents. Similar registries are

---

9. See *Getting a National Perspective on Land Use Issues,* Publication No. 267, (Washington, D.C.: League of Women Voters Education Fund, 1973). See also *Land Use,* Publication No. 485 (Washington, D.C.: League of Women Voters Education Fund, 1974).

10. See Milton Kotler and Greta Smith, *Handbook on Advisory Neighborhood Commissions* (Washington, D.C.: Institute for Neighborhood Studies, 1976).

operated as part of neighborhood planning programs in Portland, Oregon, Indianapolis, and Cincinnati.[11]

Voluntary registries of interested individuals are also used frequently. For example, in Fairfax County, Virginia, the county government publishes the *Weekly Agenda,* a popular version of the official county register, which includes notices of all meetings, forums, hearings, and other county proceedings in a simple, understandable, newspaper-type format. The *Agenda* is mailed to citizens on an open registry list and is also distributed through libraries, county offices, and schools. The *Agenda* offers names and telephone numbers of county officials so citizens know whom to call to get further information or arrange to present testimony. In essence, the registry distribution is a device for insuring that at least the most concerned citizens in each community know what issues are pending and what the stakes are.

The mass mailing approach is an expansion of the registry concept. For example, in December 1972, Vermont Environmental Board, in cooperation with the Vermont Natural Resources Council (VNRC), mailed to every household in Vermont a newsprint copy of the draft land use plans mandated by the state's Act 250.[12] Subsequently, VNRC also undertook two supplementary mailings to special audiences. One mailing was directed to 426 known environmental "activists" who had previously indicated a desire for more detailed information about statewide land use issues. These activists were sent a copy of the final detailed draft of the Land Use Capability and Development Plan, plus a list of legislators they could contact.

The second special mailing was sent to 1,200 "inactive" citizens—primarily blue-collar workers chosen from the ranks of the state AFL-CIO. These individuals were sent an informational letter on Vermont land use plans from EPIC and the AFL-CIO and a survey questionnaire through which they could express their preferences.

Analysis of response to these efforts indicates that these mass mailings could have been more effective if they had been more appropriately tailored to the needs and capabilities of each audience. For example, in a statewide sample survey conducted in May 1973, five

---

11. Center for Governmental Studies, *Neighborhood Decentralization Newsletter* (March 1974), p. 7.

12. Details on the Vermont Environmental Board effort may be found in Anthony Scoville and Adrian Noad, *Citizen Participation in State Government* (Montpelier, Vt.: Environmental Planning Information Center, Final Report to NSF-RANN, November 1973).

months after the mailings, only 39 percent of the general public remembered having received the draft land use plans in the mail.[13] Of these individuals, 50 percent considered the material "useful." By contrast, in a special survey, 46 percent of the "activists" remembered having received the Land Use Capability and Development Plan and 80 percent considered it "useful." Thus, while a copy of the formal plan may have been appropriate for known active citizens, some type of special illustrated brochure or newspaper might have been more useful for the general public.

One way of improving the impact of mass mailings is to combine them with public information meetings. An excellent example of this approach is the district appraisal program developed in Toronto.[14] This program is unusual in both the comprehensiveness and specificity of information provided.

The Toronto Planning Board periodically undertakes land use appraisals in each of the twenty-five planning districts into which the city is divided. These district appraisals establish guidelines for the future development of each area within the general context of overall city development policy.

The initial stage in the appraisal process is the preparation of a draft plan for each district, based on preliminary land use surveys. A short version of the draft plan is then sent to every household, business establishment, citizen association, and property owner within the given district. Also enclosed is a schedule of public information meetings, which are held in every neighborhood of the district.

At each of the public meetings, the impact of the proposed plan on the neighborhood as a whole is examined by the planning staff. The informational effort is then carried one step further by dividing the neighborhood audience into five or six smaller discussion groups, chaired by a citizen and a senior planning officer. Each group examines how the proposed plan will affect its own subneighborhood; maps and charts are made available to aid in this exercise.

Based on experience with a large number of district appraisals, the head of the Toronto Planning Board asserts that between 8 percent and 10 percent of the total adult population in a district will attend one or more planning meetings. This figure typically includes

13. Adrian Noad and Anthony Scoville, "Citizen Attitudes on State Government and Citizen Participation," in Scoville and Noad, *Citizen Participation in State Government,* pp. 36–37.

14. See W. Clark, "The District Appraisal Approach," in *Planning 1965* (Chicago: American Society of Planning Officials, 1965).

participation by residents of more than one-third of the owner-occupied housing units in the district—an extraordinary turnout for citizen involvement in land use governance. Thus, while the Toronto approach is obviously expensive and time consuming, the planning board chairman concludes:

Our experience over the past few years has convinced us that the results to date amply justify the time, the organizational effort, and the money spent on public consultation and citizen participation in our district appraisal approach to planning. We believe the results (of the effort) are lasting and cumulative.[15]

While every jurisdiction may not have the financial and technical resources necessary for a similar effort, the Toronto approach deserves serious consideration as an outstanding example of providing current policy information.

As an alternative or supplement to the use of mailings or meetings, one method that has received increasing attention as a means of informing citizens is the permanent planning information center, which mounts continuous exhibitions on proposed plans and projects.[16] This concept has been implemented on a centralized basis in Lakewood, Colorado. There, a city hall municipal information center presents audiovisual displays on all current plans and projects for the city.[17] Similarly, the city of Minneapolis has implemented the concept of satellite planning centers, which operate outside the central planning office.[18] Each satellite center is staffed by two full-time planners and two paraprofessionals from the neighborhood. The paraprofessionals aid in "translating" plans and projects into understandable terms for neighborhood residents.

To expand the reach of the planning information center, mobile exhibitions are often used. For example, in Lakewood, informational materials developed by the central information center are also used

---

15. Ibid, p. 168.

16. Two of the most prominent advocates of planning information centers are Melville Branch, "Continuous Master City Planning," in Ira Robinson, ed., *Decision-Making in Urban Planning* (Beverly Hills, Cal.: Sage Publications, 1972); and Alfred Kahn, *Neighborhood Information Centers: A Study and Some Proposals* (New York: Columbia University School of Social Work, 1966).

17. The Lakewood approach is discussed in Management Information Service, *Public Involvement in Local Government in the 1970s* (Washington, D.C.: International City Management Association, 1974).

18. See M. McNeese, "Neighborhood Planning Agencies," 38 *Planning* 232–238 (1972).

in a mobile planning office that travels to neighborhoods engaged in land use controversies.

In Minneapolis, the Model Cities Communications Center operates a mobile van that provides detailed information on proposed plans and projects in the model neighborhood through movies, displays, and slide shows. The van also is used as a travelling office for local aldermen so that citizens can voice their views about land use and community development issues directly to elected officials.[19]

Perhaps the most elaborate exercise in this approach to providing current information took place recently in Coventry, England. An exhibition on the proposed "structure plan" for the city was set up in a large bus.[20] For three months, this bus toured different neighborhoods, adapting its displays to highlight the particular impacts on each area. Copies of land use surveys and plans, brochures, and questionnaires were also available.

The Coventry bus also became an information center for public meetings on the structure plan held in each neighborhood. Some 4,300 adults visited the bus during a three-month period of intensive meetings. During a two-week period in which the bus visited secondary schools, more than 1,200 students per day toured the exhibition. Of course, these raw statistics do not indicate anything about the quality of the information obtained or the use to which it was put, but the effort to reach large numbers of people with "localized" information on the implications of proposed land use plans must be considered a success in terms of attracting an audience.

PARTICIPATION OPPORTUNITIES

Defining Policy Options

What techniques can be used to identify the distinctive policy options that enjoy significant citizen support? Traditional methods are advisory groups and public meetings or workshops. In recent years, there have been many efforts to improve the use of these basic techniques, as well as intensive experimentation with innovative approaches.

---

19. See Diana Klugman, "Communications and Community," 11 *Nation's Cities*, 36–38 (1973).

20. See *Structure Plan 1973: Statement on Public Participation* (Conventry, England: The City Council, 1973).

Citizen Advisory Groups. Advisory groups have long been a means of clarifying public opinion on community problems. This type of body also has been consistently criticized as unrepresentative of the full range of community interests and as excessively vulnerable to manipulation by administrative staff.[21] However, many communities are currently making vigorous efforts to address these problems.

In Winston-Salem, North Carolina, for example, the city council has established a series of citizen policy planning committees focusing on different aspects of urban development and land use. To insure broad opportunity for the identification of different interests and preferences, Winston-Salem has developed an elaborate set of guidelines for advisory committee selection.[22] These provisions are as follows:

1. Membership of each committee will be between ten and thirty in number, large enough to prevent domination by special interests, small enough to be effective.
2. Committees will have a balance between consumers and neighborhoods on the one hand and special interests on the other.
3. Members will be selected by one of the following methods:
   • selection by neighborhood councils and special interest groups directly;
   • or appointment by city and county councils, based upon nominations from neighborhood councils and special interest groups.
   Neighborhood councils will include all residents of the neighborhood who wish to participate. Neighborhood councils will select a small slate of officers and representatives to planning committees annually at neighborhood meetings.
4. No individual will serve on more than one policy planning committee.
5. Committees can include a small number of additional

21. Roberta Sigel, "Citizen's Advisory Groups," 6 *Nation's Cities,* 15–21 (1968); Pierre Clavel, "Planners and Citizen Boards: Some Applications of Social Theory to the Problem of Implementation," 34 *American Institute of Planners Journal,* 130–139 (1968); David Brown, "The Management of Advisory Committees: An Assignment for the '70s," 32 *Public Administration Review,* 334–342 (1972); Dorothy Kiester, "Citizen Boards: Do They Serve a Purpose," 40 *Popular Government,* 40–43 (1975).

22. The Winston-Salem program is described in Management Information Service, *Public Involvement in Local Government in the 1970s* (Washington, D.C.: International City Management Association, 1974) pp. 10–11.

members who may be added directly by the city and county councils to prevent an imbalance of race, sex, or some other significant characteristic.

Through this hybrid selection system—similar to that implemented in other cities such as Cincinnati, Ohio, and Texarkana, Texas—it is hoped that advisory committees can be reinvigorated as lively forums for a broad range of views on policy issues.

As an alternative to the improvement of selection procedures, several jurisdictions are experimenting with the *election* of citizen advisory groups—typically on a neighborhood basis. As previously noted, the District of Columbia has elected Advisory Neighborhood Commissions to review and comment on all proposed plans and projects affecting their neighborhoods.[23] Similarly, Dayton, Ohio, recently set up six elected Neighborhood Priority Boards.[24] In that jurisdiction, city commissions routinely refer all proposed zoning and land use changes to the relevant priority board for commentary; planning specialists from the city then aid the boards in evaluating proposals. Simliar approaches to the election of citizen advisory groups have been implemented in Birmingham, Alabama; Honolulu, Hawaii; New York City; and other jurisdictions.[25]

There is a legitimate question about whether the election of advisory groups results in a more representative expression of citizen preferences. In the election for Dayton's priority boards in December 1971, only 13 percent of eligible voters cast ballots; the following year there was an even smaller turnout. In the District of Columbia's citizen advisory group elections of February 1976, voter turnout was less than 10 percent. Thus, unless voter interest can be increased, exclusive reliance on elections as a mechanism of choosing advisory committees seems unwise.

A third approach to the selection of citizen advisory groups involves granting some type of official status and role to established citizen organizations, whether on a neighborhood or special interest basis. This approach has been implemented, for example, in Salem,

---

23. Kotler and Smith, *Handbook on Advisory Neighborhood Commissions* (Washington, D.C.: Institute for Neighborhood Studies, 1976).

24. Earl Sterzer, "Neighborhood Grant Program Lets Citizens Decide," 53 *Public Management,* (1971).

25. See Center for Governmental Studies, *Charter Language and Ordinances on Neighborhood Decentralization* (Washington, D.C.: Center for Governmental Studies, 1974).

Oregon, where neighborhood groups are officially recognized as advisory groups on land use, transportation, and other development matters if they meet certain criteria of openness and representativeness.[26] Similarly, the city of San Diego charters citizen groups as official advisory planning bodies for their area if they meet a set of conditions.[27] This approach shows much promise, but it also contains potential pitfalls. Unless the functioning of chartered groups is carefully monitored, there is always a danger that the interests and preferences of those segments of the affected public that do not choose to join or participate will not be considered in the definition of policy alternatives.

Beyond making advisory committees more representative of affected citizens, several jurisdictions have experimented with efforts to provide the groups with a more central role in the definition of policy alternatives. For example, several jurisdictions have used citizens as active coworkers in the preparation of plans and project designs.

In Cincinnati, this "task force" approach has been used in planning for the redevelopment of low-income neighborhoods. The prototype of this program was the West End Task Force, established in 1966.[28] Appointed by the city manager with the concurrence of the city council, the task force consisted of eighteen members, selected from neighborhood citizen associations, property-owners' and business organizations, and city agencies dealing with such matters as public works and housing. Working under the direction of the city's planning department, the task force met every two weeks for several years, completing a detailed work program of surveys, preliminary planning, and detailed project design. The result was a draft comprehensive plan for the West End.

In Washington, D.C., the task force approach has been used to plan for commercial development in and around proposed subway stations of the Metro system. The prototype task force was established in the Friendship Heights section—a high-income residential area near the Maryland border. In 1973, the Office of Planning and Management of the District government invited the area's citizens associations to establish an advisory board that could work directly

26. City of Salem, *Neighborhood Planning in Salem, Oregon* (Salem, Ore.: Community Development Department, City of Salem, March 26, 1975).

27. See Douglas Harman, *Citizen Involvement in Urban Planning: The San Diego Experiment* (San Diego: Public Affairs Research Institute, San Diego College, 1968).

28. See M. Gieser, "Planning with the People," 25 *Journal of Housing,* 298–301 (1968).

with city agencies in exploring options for the area. Over the course of a year, a broadly representative group of citizens worked with planners to produce an action agenda—a Plan for Friendship Heights—that recommended both drastic downzoning of certain properties in the area and concentrated development in others.[29] After endorsement by all local citizen associations, the zoning recommendations contained in the plan were adopted by the city's planning commission in 1974.

Public Meetings and Workshops. Several communities have attempted to improve the usefulness of public meetings and workshops by using more systematic techniques to analyze citizen viewpoints. In Boulder, Colorado, for example, the Boulder Area Growth Study Commission used the "nominal group process" to identify citizen perceptions of the consequences of community growth and how to deal with those effects.[30] Workshop participants in Boulder were divided into several small groups of six to nine people. Members of each group were then asked to spend thirty minutes to one hour on written responses identifying both the desirable and undesirable consequences of growth in the community and options for dealing with the undesirable aspects. At the conclusion of this phase, a group leader transcribed all the problems identified onto a master list. This list was then discussed for thirty minutes to one hour, during which time group participants were urged to elaborate on and defend particular items, make additions, or suggest deletions. Each group then voted on which items were the most crucial consequences of growth and which the most feasible policy options. All the groups then met together and the votes of each group were reported to the entire audience. A final vote was taken, which served as basic input for the deliberations of the policy-making body.

This type of process may seem extremely involved and time consuming, but the final vote provided a clearer ranking of priorities and preferences among a substantial group of citizen participants than would have been possible through discussion alone. Similar types of structured small-group discussion techniques—e.g., "Delphi" and

---

29. Task Force on Friendship Heights, *Plan for the Friendship Heights Area of the District of Columbia* (Washington, D.C.: District of Columbia Office of Planning and Management, 1973).

30. See Boulder Area Growth Study Commission, *Exploring Options for the Future: Volume I—Final Report* (Boulder, Colo.: Boulder Area Growth Study Commission, 1973). On the technique of the "nominal group process," see A. Delbecq and A. Van de Ven, "A Group Process Model for Problem Identification and Program Planning," 7 *Journal of Applied Behavioral Science,* 466–492 (1971).

"Charette"—have been used in other communities to clarify policy options in land use workshops and public forums.[31]

The state of Oregon used a simpler but related approach to analyzing workshop input. The state's Land Conservation and Development Commission held a series of twenty-eight public workshops across the state to obtain initial public input in the development of statewide planning goals and guidelines.[32] More than 3,000 citizens attended these workshops, where sessions were structured around six discussion questions presented in a brief questionnaire that all participants were asked to complete. The questionnaires were then systematically analyzed to highlight the major options and alternatives that citizens identified. Results were developed both for the entire state and for each of seven regions. At the end of this process, the Oregon commission had a detailed understanding of the major issues and options identified by workshop participants. A similar approach to the systematic analysis of public preferences has been developed by the U.S. Forest Service in its large-scale planning exercises.[33]

Other Approaches. In addition to improving these traditional mechanisms of determining policy options, many communities have been testing new, more flexible approaches to the task of defining policy options. One of the most prominent of these is encouraging and/or subsidizing *alternative plans*—i.e., plans that reflect the uncompromised views of a particular individual or citizen groups.[34] These

---

31. On the Delphi method in general, see Normal Dalkey, *The Delphi Method: An Experimental Study of Group Opinion,* Publication No. RM-5888—PR (Santa Monica: The Rand Corporation, 1969); and Harold Sackman, *Delphi Critique: Expert Opinion Forecasting and the Group Process* (Lexington, Mass.: D.C. Heath, 1975). For applications of Delphi to land use planning and regulation, see Osborn Erwin, "The Delphi Method: Some Applications to Local Planning," 32 *The Tennessee Planner,* 34–51 (1974); Donald Molnor and Marshall Kammerud, "Developing Priorities for Improving the Urban Social Environment: A Use of Delphi," 9 *Socio-Economic Planning Sciences,* 25–29 (1975). On Charrette methodology see Dale Chase, *The Charette Process,* (Washington, D.C.: Office of Education, DHEW, 1973). On the application of charrette technique to land use planning, see Sherwin Kalm, *Baltimore Charrette: Experiment in Planning an Urban High School* (New York: Educational Facilities Library, New York University, 1969).

32. The Oregon workshops are described in *A Report on People and the Land Public Workshops* (Salem, Ore.: Oregon Department of Land Conservation and Development, July 1974).

33. See John C. Hendee et al., *Public Involvement and the Forest Service* (Washington, D.C.: U.S. Forest Service, May 1973), chs. IV and V.

34. On the concept of alternative planning, see Paul Davidoff, "Advocacy and Pluralism in Planning," 31 *American Institute of Planners Journal* 331–338 (1965); and Donald Mozzrotti, "The Underlying Assumptions of Advocacy Planning: Pluralism and Reform," 35 *American Institute of Planners Journal,* 96–101 (1969).

plans, in turn, can be used to help determine the agenda for the official planning process.

In middle- and upper-income areas, alternative plans have frequently been produced by citizen groups themselves, without reliance on external professional or technical assistance. For example, in the Friendship Heights section of Montgomery County, Maryland, a coalition of neighborhood citizen associations—relying on the expertise of its own members—produced a highly detailed, technically proficient alternative plan for developing the area. The plan recommended less high-density commercial development than proposed by area developers. In the face of intense political activism, the Montgomery County Council eventually accepted many of the recommendations made in the citizens' plan.

A similar example is the alternative plan produced by the Glover Park-Burleith Citizens' Association for the Wisconsin Avenue area of Washington, D.C. With the encouragement of the D.C. government, this group developed a schematic plan that produced two results. First, immediate action on zoning variance requests for the area was forestalled. Second, the alternative plan has become the agenda upon which the city is basing its own planning for the area.

In lower income areas, on the other hand, alternative planning has usually been conducted within the context of "advocacy planning centers" financed by the community action and model cities programs.[35] Citizen groups in these areas rarely enjoy a high level of technical expertise among their members. Thus, to produce a plan or project design outside official channels, they must rely on the technical assistance of advocacy planners. Some typical advocacy planning centers are the Metro Link Community Design Center in New Orleans, the Architects Renewal Committee in Harlem, and Urban Planning Aid in Boston.[36] The last group helped produce alternative transportation plans for citizen antihighway groups in the Boston area. The Architects Renewal Committee, working with several citizen groups, produced an alternative plan for the site of a major state office

35. On advocacy planning centers for the poor, see Paul Davidoff et al., "Suburban Action: Advocate Planning for an Open Society," 36 *American Institute of Planners Journal* 12–21 (1970); Marshall Kaplan, "Advocacy and the Urban Poor," 35 *American Institute of Planners Journal*, 96–101 (1969); and Lise Peattie, "Reflections on Advocacy Planning," 34 *American Institute of Planners Journal*, 80–88 (1968).

36. See E. Blecher, *Advocacy Planning for Urban Development* (New York: Praeger, 1971), and "Symposium on Advocacy Planning in Low-Income Neighborhoods," in *Planning 1970* (Chicago: American Society of Planning Officials, 1970).

building in Harlem. That plan eventually led to major changes in the project's development. Metro Link has worked with the New Orleans Tenants Organization to produce an alternative to the housing authority's plan for redevelopment of the Desire housing project.

An alternative plan may play a useful role in a program of citizen involvement as a detailed expression of views by particular individuals or groups of citizens. However, alternative planning should certainly not be relied upon as the central component of citizen participation. Planners and administrators have an obligation to identify a broader range of citizen interests and preferences than those presented by one particular group. Alternative planning must thus be balanced with additional participatory mechanisms.

One of the most innovative approaches to clarifying policy options is the use of gaming and simulation.[37] A recent effort to use simulation in land use planning was conducted by Champaign-Urbana, Illinois, in cooperation with the University of Illinois.[38] In the last decade, the fate of Boneyard Creek, a small, flood-prone stream, has been a significant issue in this Illinois community. To identify feasible options, the Computer-Based Education Laboratory of the University of Illinois developed a Boneyard Creek simulation program for use with the Plato IV teaching computer. The program consisted of basic information about the controversy and a series of development scenarios and alternatives. More than 100 prominent community residents were invited to work through this program through individual remote access terminals. Ninety-one citizens completed the program and filled out an evaluation questionnaire. Of the ninety-one, eighty-four indicated interest in working on another community issue using the computer and expressed willingness to invite a neighbor to participate.

In Saratoga, New York, a noncomputerized simulation game was used to define plan alternatives for downtown redevelopment.[39] Randomly selected citizen participants from the affected area were

---

37. On the use of gaming and simulation in urban land use planning and regulation, see Marshall Whithed, "The Use of Simulation Techniques in Urban Planning Analysis and Teaching," 8 *Studies of Comparative Local Government,* 22–34 (1974); and *Simulation/Gaming News,* No. 10, 1974.

38. The Boneyard Creek simulation program is described in Stuart Umpleby, "Citizen Sampling Simulations: A Method for Involving the Public in Local Planning," 1 *Policy Sciences,* 361–375 (1970).

39. On the Saratoga experiment, see Ben Griffin and Tom Moyer, "Saratoga's the Name of the Game," *Planning* 11–12 (1975).

encouraged to design a new vision of Saratoga with the aid of a large-scale model of the downtown area. Political and economic assumptions implicit in the model were periodically changed as part of the gaming exercise. The results of the gaming were recorded systematically and incorporated in the proposed plan of action prepared by the city government.

A final method of defining feasible policy alternatives, one that has been receiving increasing attention, is the systematic distribution of successive draft plans to a panel of citizen reviewers. This procedure derives from European administrative practice. In Sweden, for example, land use plans and evaluations of major projects are routinely submitted for review and comment to a wide range of interested and knowledgeable parties, such as special interest groups, citizen associations, and political organizations.[40] These parties have a specified period of time to review and comment upon the proposals. Upon receipt of these submissions, the planning or regulatory agency typically prepares a summary digest of major and minor criticisms; this digest serves as a principal source for revising and modifying plans.

In the United States, the review and comment procedure has been used in the coastal zone planning process in California.[41] Copies of successive drafts of coastal zone plan elements were circulated to review panels across the state for review and comment. All responses were systematically analyzed and digested into summary statements of public preferences, which the planning staff then used to develop the final proposed plan.

Estimating Aggregate Preferences

Once policy options and basic positions have been clearly defined, how can opinions within the affected public as a whole be accurately and meaningfully assessed?

The traditional minimum method of securing communitywide

---

40. Swedish administrative practice on citizen involvement is described in Shirley Passow, "Stockholm's Planners Discover People Power," 39 *American Institute of Planners Journal,* 23–34 (1973).

41. See Judy Rosener, "The California Experience: Emerging Issues and Research Needs," paper presented to the 1975 National Conference on Public Administration, Chicago, Ill., April 1975. A detailed discussion of the California citizen involvement program may be found in Nelson Rosenbaum, *State Land Use Controls: An Evaluation of Citizen Involvement in Decision Making* (Washington, D.C.: The Urban Institute, forthcoming).

comment is the public hearing. For many years, the public hearing was the only widely used method of citizen participation in the processes of land use governance, and it is still the most common technique of citizen involvement programs.

The public hearing has been vigorously criticized for its lack of both flexibility and representativeness.[42] To a large extent, this dissatisfaction arises from the use of public hearings as the primary vehicle for citizen participation. Clearly, because of limitations on the number who can meaningfully participate and the legal formality of the proceedings, public hearings cannot carry the main load of estimating aggregate community preferences. Rather, the public hearing is most useful as a "summing up," or formal conclusion to the decision-making process. The hearing is a symbolic opportunity for individuals and organizations to go on the record with their final criticisms and suggestions.

This is not to say, however, that there is no need to improve the conduct of public hearings. There are many ways to improve hearing procedures, ranging from holding multiple decentralized hearings to allowing greater interchange between citizen and public officials. A number of jurisdictions across the nation are experimenting with such techniques.[43]

One of the most direct and useful alternatives for assessing preference patterns among large populations is the sample survey. Since the 1930s, surveys of attitudes toward political personalities and problems have become commonplace in American life. In the area of land use, however, the use of surveys has often been accompanied by considerable dissatisfaction. One reason is that survey sampling is often unrepresentative and unsophisticated, particularly in terms of identifying the views of politically important subgroups of the affected public. Second, survey questions are often simplistic and unrealistic, failing to portray the true complexity of choice among competing policy options.

One survey that creatively addressed the sampling problem was

---

42. For a review of the major criticisms, see American Society of Planning Officials, *Public Hearing, Controversy, and the Written Response,* Planning Advisory Service Report 240 (Chicago, ASPO, 1968).

43. See, for example, Clifford Goodall, "How to Conduct a Public Hearing," 38 *The Maine Townsman* 17 (1976); Anthony Scoville and Adrian Noad, *Citizen Participation in State Government* (Montpelier, Vt.: Vermont Natural Resources Council, 1970), Final Report to NSF-RANN, Chs 2 and 3.

recently conducted by Utah State University.[44] Utah is divided into seven planning districts, based upon major distinctions of climate, geography, and economic development; these divisions are critical in the state political process. In contemplating the potential usefulness of a statewide survey on land use attitudes and preferences, researchers at Utah State decided that the results would be most meaningful to decision makers if preference patterns could be assessed within each district as well as in the state as a whole. This could not be accomplished by standard area probability sampling methodology because planning districts varied widely in population. Thus, there would not be enough respondents from particular districts to generalize for that specific area.

The solution was a disproportional stratified sample, taking approximately equal numbers of respondents from each district. In this way, the researchers had enough respondents to generalize about each district, and they could still draw a representative portrait of statewide opinion through special weighting of the disproportional sample. This technique thus allowed meaningful generalization by district as well as aggregation on a statewide level.

Disproportional sampling and quota weighting are useful techniques in any jurisdiction in which simple random or area probability sampling would not pick up sufficient numbers of particular groups (geographical, racial, socioeconomic, etc.) to permit accurate analysis of group preferences.

With regard to questionnaire design, one of the more valuable recent efforts is the priority evaluator approach developed by researchers at Social and Community Planning Research in London.[45] This technique is designed to overcome the problem of "nonattitudes" by presenting respondents with a realistic appreciation of the trade-offs involved in a choice between competing policy options. As used in a number of studies of environmental problems in greater London, the technique presents each respondent with a set of scales that detail, in both words and pictures, the various trade-offs in a particular policy decision. For example, a survey on transportation pre-

44. See H. Bylund and H. Geertsen, *Public Views on Land Use Planning in Utah* (Logan, Utah: Utah State University, 1974). A general discussion of the importance of disaggregation in surveys is found in N. Johnson and E. Ward, "Citizen Information Systems: Using Technology to Extend the Dialogue Between Citizens and their Government," 19 *Management Science* 21–34 (1972).

45. G. Hoinville, "Evaluating Community Preferences," 3 *Environment and Planning* 33–50 (1971).

sents scales dealing with such matters as travel time, cost, and degree of crowding. Respondents are then asked to indicate their relative priorities among these values by trading off given quantities of one vis-a-vis another under a set of groundrules established by the researcher. Each respondent's "optimal mix" of environmental values represents a particular preference that can then be related to the specific policy options under consideration by an agency. This technique represents a substantial advance over the direct question approach because it induces the respondent to think in specific quantitative terms instead of vague generalized preferences.

Another direct means of attempting to ascertain the distribution of public preferences on land use policy issues is the advisory referendum. This approach is typically used when decision makers wish a more formal expression of preferences than a survey provides. An example is the referendum held in Petaluma, California, in June 1973. In 1971 and 1972, the Petaluma City Council adopted a series of increasingly stringent growth control measures, culminating in passage of the Residential Development Control System in August 1972. To a large extent, this legislative action was guided by the results of previous citizen involvement exercises, particularly the recommendations of a citizen study commission, the Petaluma Planning Conference, and the results of a questionnaire distributed to 10,000 city residents. However, since the control system aroused such heated opposition from developers and some citizens, the planning commission and city council decided to seek a more formal expression of public attitudes about the land use controls as a basis for future action. An advisory referendum was therefore conducted; those voting approved the control system by a margin of more than four to one (4,444 to 953).

Despite the relatively low cost of advisory referenda and the attractiveness of a formal expression of preferences, there are potential difficulties with this method. First, citizen choice in a referendum is realistically limited to approval or disapproval of a single policy option. This contrasts with the flexibility of survey research, in which a broad variety of policy options may be presented to the respondent for comment and reaction. Second, because voter turnout in referenda is characteristically low and advisory referenda are particularly subject to apathy, the results may reflect the preferences of only a small proportion of the affected public.

In recent years, considerable attention has been devoted to the possibility of combining the features of advisory referenda and surveys through the technological capabilities of two-way cable television and telephone hookups. Through television, a larger number of options and a good deal of background information can be presented to potential respondents. Through a two-way cable or telephone linkage, voters can record their preferences easily and conveniently, counteracting the prevalent disinclination to use traditional voting procedures.

An experimental version of such a system is currently operating in San Jose, California.[46] Communication from government to citizens is conducted through newspapers and mailed leaflets as well as television. To "vote" through the telephone system, respondents first dial a special number that connects to an automatic recorder. They then dial in an identification code (which insures that each person votes only once), an issue number, and a number indicating the citizen's preference on the issue. The recorded information is periodically processed by computer to determine the distribution of public preferences on an issue.

More than 5,000 citizens have participated in the "Televote System." A sample survey of participants found that 95 percent evaluated the technical aspects of the system favorably, and 80 percent thought the system kept them in closer touch with government. The flexibility in presenting alternatives and the ease of voting that this approach incorporates are important technical advances. Similar experiments are currently underway in New York City; Santa Barbara, California; Troy, New York; and other cities across the country.[47]

ACCOUNTABILITY TECHNIQUES

Explaining Policy Decisions

Under the typical procedural mandates of administrative procedure, freedom of information, and sunshine laws, final plans and orders are usually circulated to all officially recognized "interested parties" and public access to all records and transcripts of decision-making bodies is provided. These procedures are, however, essentially passive, in that they imposed no obligation on an agency to explain directly the reasons for its actions and decisions.

---

46. Vincent Campbell, *The Televote System: Final Report* (Palo Alto, Cal.: American Institutes for Research, 1974).

47. Amitai Etzioni, *Minerva: A Study in Participatory Technology* (New York: Center for Policy Research, 1972); William Ewald Jr., *Access: The Santa Barbara Regional Pilot Process* (Washington, D.C.: National Science Foundation, 1973); and Thomas P. Sheridan, "Citizen Feedback: New Technology for Social Choice," 73 *Technology Review* (1971).

One approach that carries accountability a step further has been undertaken in Coventry, England. As part of its public participation program under the Town and Country Planning Act of 1971, the Coventry city council submitted copies of its corporate planning surveys and draft structure plan to a large number of local conservation societies, taxpayer associations, special interest groups, and individual citizens. More than 1,500 comments were received. The city council then directed the planning department to respond explicitly to every comment and suggestion, stating the official response and the rationale for changing or not changing the plan. The record of these comments and responses was subsequently published as part of the official documentation of the planning process.[48]

The state of Oregon implemented a different approach to expanding accountability. Upon completion of a year-long process of public hearings, workshops, committee meetings, and other means of soliciting citizen participation, the State Land Conservation and Development Commission held a special public "mark-up session" to reach its decisions on statewide planning goals and guidelines and to explain them to citizens. The session was open to questions from the audience on the rationale for particular decisions. After the mark-up session, the commission printed 20,000 copies of a tabloid newspaper presenting and explaining the goals and guidelines. These newspapers were mailed to every individual and group that participated in the decision-making process, and were also distributed through schools and private organizations.[49]

A final example of expanded accountability is the procedure adopted by the California Coastal Zone Conservation Commission. In the course of the planning process, extensive citizen commentary was received on many different aspects of the preliminary coastal plan. Because of the volume of commentary, individual replies were not feasible. Thus, the commission staff prepared a special systematic summary of changes in the preliminary plan that were made in response to citizen input. This special summary was then distributed to all citizens who reviewed and commented on successive drafts of

48. See *Structure Plan 1973: Statement on Public Participation* (Conventry, England: The City Council, 1973).

49. Oregon Land Conservation and Development Commission, *Statewide Planning Goals and Guidelines* (Salem, Oregon: LCDC, December 1974). For a comprehensive discussion of the Oregon experience, see Nelson Rosenbaum, *State Land Use Controls: An Evaluation of Citizen Involvement in Decision Making* (Washington, D.C.: The Urban Institute, forthcoming).

the preliminary plan, as well as to any other citizen who requested a copy.

The common element in each of these approaches is respect for the intelligence and contributions of the public. By demonstrating such respect, administrative agencies can assure the public that our democracy works fairly and responsively.

Testing Policy Decisions

The primary means of testing most local land use decisions is review by the legislative body of the jurisdiction involved. For example, comprehensive plans, zoning ordinances and maps, and subdivision plats must all be submitted for local legislative approval under the typical state enabling statute. However, many individuals and citizen groups have expressed discontent with the rubber-stamp quality of local legislative review, or they have faulted the composition of local legislative bodies as unfairly biased toward development interests.

At higher levels of government—regional, state, and federal— legislative review of administrative decisions is only rarely available.

Notwithstanding efforts to improve local legislative review or to stimulate such review at higher levels of government, what alternative means of testing the fairness and responsiveness of administrative decisions can be used in a citizen involvement program? Two basic methods of testing land use decisions are referenda and judicial review.

Referenda. A referendum is the most direct means of testing the correspondence between public preferences and public policy. Referenda have been employed in many jurisdictions to test general land use policy. For example, in Boca Raton, Florida, citizen pressure induced the city council to place the issue of growth control before the voters as a charter referendum. In this case, the electorate approved a controversial "growth cap" policy that limits the number of residential units that can be built in the municipality. In a citizen-initiated referendum in Nevada, voters defeated a growth policy act passed by the legislature. In Boulder, Colorado, the land use plan prepared by the Boulder Area Growth Study Commission was submitted to referendum and approved by the voters.

Referenda have also been utilized in land use decision making on a project-by-project and decision-by-decision basis. In Maryland, for example, a special act of the legislature authorized a binding referendum on the issue of building an oil refinery in St. Mary's County,

Maryland. Reversing prior approval by county administrative agencies, county voters decisively defeated the refinery proposal by a margin of more than two to one, with more than 60 percent of registered voters casting ballots.

Many states allow municipalities to conduct "zoning by referendum," in which registered voters must approve all proposed zoning changes. In New Hampshire, for example, a local referendum defeated a proposed rezoning that would have accommodated a major oil refinery in the Durham area.

The referendum is clearly attractive as a direct and simple test of popular response to land use decisions, but there is a need for some caution in its authorization. Where land use decisions by administrative agencies are clearly quasi-legislative in character and are submitted to legislatures for review and approval, the authorization of referenda (either by specific legislative act or by citizen initiative under general constitutional authorization) is clearly justified. Citizen review of legislative enactments is a fundamental principle of American democratic practice at the state and local levels of government.

On the other hand, serious questions arise with the use of referenda for review of specific projects and zoning decisions. The application of the law to specific pieces of property requires safeguards of due process and equal protection. Many commentators have questioned whether zoning by referendum provides adequate guarantees of equity and fairness to the affected property owner. Indeed, a number of state supreme courts have banned zoning by referendum.[50] The point here is not to argue that referenda on specific projects and zoning decisions are always inappropriate, but rather to stress that the technique presents difficult questions of due process. Elected officials should be aware of those problems before authorizing or encouraging use of the referendum.

---

50. For a comprehensive review of state court decisions on zoning by referendum, see Craig Oren, "The Initiative and Referendum's Use in Zoning," 64 *California Law Review* 74 (1974). A popular treatment is found in Randall Scott, "Zoning by Initiative and Referendum," *Urban Land,* February, March, and April 1974.

During its 1975–1976 term, the U.S. Supreme Court accepted a case involving zoning referenda. In *City of Eastlake* v. *Forest City Enterprises,* the Court upheld the validity of mandatory referenda on zoning actions in a municipality. The core of the decision was the majority's finding that the zoning decision at issue—a variance for the construction of high-rise apartments—was a legislative rather than adjudicative or administrative action. In general, the state courts have taken a more narrow view of what constitutes legislative action and is thus appropriate for referendum. The Supreme Court's broad categorization of legislative action will have some influence in the state courts, but will not necessarily result in a reversal or denial of state-imposed restrictions on the use of referenda.

Judical Review. Access to judicial review of administrative decisions has traditionally been available to "interested parties" in land
use matters—i.e., those citizens with some direct property stake in
the decision or those to whom the administrative agency grants recognition in its proceedings. In recent years, however, access to judicial review has been greatly expanded by both general procedural
statutes and the specific provisions of more substantive statutes.

Perhaps the most important breakthrough in providing citizen access to the courts was the National Environmental Policy Act (NEPA)
of 1970. This law provided judicial review to any individual citizen or group alleging inadequacies in the required environmental impact statement. Beyond its impact in spurring citizen-initiated litigation at the federal level, NEPA has also spawned progeny at the state
and local levels, beginning with the Michigan Environmental Protection Act of 1970.[51] State and local statutes have been used vigorously
to test land use decisions. In California, for example, a state court recently invalidated the Los Angeles County General Plan on the basis
of an inadequate environmental impact statement.

Citizen groups have also been quite active in using judicial review authorized by specific land use statutes. For example, power
plant siting decisions in several states have been challenged in court
under review provisions of new siting legislation.

The use of judicial review is quite attractive to citizens because of
its direct and forceful nature. Like a referendum, such review
preempts the immediate implementation of decisions and provides
the potential for total reversal. Citizen groups have won many notable
victories during the past decade in overturning what they perceived
as unfair and unresponsive decisions. However, there are also some
pitfalls that elected officials must contemplate in considering access
to the courts.

First, there is the inherent danger of excessive concentration of
authority in the judiciary itself. Despite the enthusiasm of some environmental advocates about judicial activism, there is a grave peril to

---

51. On citizen litigation under the National Environmental Policy Act, see Fred-
erick Anderson, *NEPA in the Courts: A Legal Analysis of the National Environmental
Policy Act* (Baltimore: Johns Hopkins University Press for Resources for the Future,
1974). The Michigan Environmental Policy Act is discussed by its author in Joseph Sax,
Defending the Environment: A Strategy for Citizen Action (New York: Knopf, 1971). A
comprehensive review of state environmental policy acts and the provisions for judicial
review contained therein is found in Kathleen Christensen et al., *State Required Impact
Evaluation of Land Developments* (Washington, D.C.: The Urban Institute, 1974), Working Paper 214–302.

the democratic process in substituting a judge's view for the judgment of the administrative agency or the legislature involved. For example, the Georgia Supreme Court recently aroused much concern by overturning a local land use decision on the basis of a substantive inquiry into the community's needs. The two dissenting justices noted:[52]

> What the court is holding is that it will now review any local zoning decision based on conflicting evidence to determine whether it bears a substantial relation to the health, safety, morality, or general welfare.
>
> The implication is that every local zoning authority in Georgia must now justify to the court every disputed zoning decision it makes.
>
> The great danger inherent in this ruling is that it will necessarily substitute the court's judgment for the local governing authority's judgment when the evidence is in conflict, as in the present case.

Of course, most judges have shied away from substantive judgments in reviewing land use controversies and have based decisions on narrower standards of procedural fairness—i.e., whether an action seems to be "arbitrary and capricious" in relation to the record, or whether it gives "adequate consideration" to all affected interests. The remedy in most cases where such a test is not met is to remand the case to the agency rather than to substitute a judicial decision. However, there is no assurance of such judicial restraint.

Second, litigation is a costly process, which makes it effectively available only to those citizens or groups enjoying extensive financial resources or access to low-cost assistance. These circumstances limit the representativeness of testing administrative decisions through the judicial process.

Finally, judicial review is extraordinarily time consuming because of the present congestion of civil cases in state and federal courts. Judicial review and appeals can easily consume several years, while costs rise and property is held in limbo. In some cases, the delays have become intolerable. For example, Congress recently limited further judicial review of the Alaska pipeline case after a protracted delay in decision making.

This is not to advocate limitation of the availability of judicial review to individuals and citizen groups. In most respects, judicial review remains the most reasonable and impartial means of testing the procedural fairness of land use decisions. However, the problems

---

52. *Ernest W. Barrett et al., Commissioners* v. *Doyle Hamby, Exr.,* 219 S. E. 2d 399, 404, Dissent of Justice Ingram and Justice Jordan.

and pitfalls should be recognized in debating the appropriate extent of reliance upon judicial review.

Other Strategies. Given the limitations of referenda and judicial review, there has been considerable interest in recent years in experimenting with alternative means of testing the fairness and responsiveness of administrative decisions.

One alternative that has attracted attention is the use of formal mediation or arbitration between administrative agencies and citizen groups. In Washington state, for example, Governor Daniel Evans appointed a team of mediators from the state university to intervene in a long-standing land use dispute between the Army Corps of Engineers and environmental organizations.[53] The objective of the appointed mediators was to arrive at a voluntary agreement between the agency and the contesting groups, one that both sides would perceive as fair and responsive. After major modifications in the initial Corps decisions, such an agreement was reached.

Mediation appears to be a promising technique for testing agency decisions because of its flexibility and relatively low cost. However, the technique does pose some potential problems. First, whose interests are represented in the mediation process? Is it only the loudest, most militant citizen groups, or is it a wide spectrum of affected citizens? Obviously, there is a potential for abuse if the mediation team itself is given carte blanche to select the parties to the testing process.

Second, because mediation is based on the prospect of voluntary agreement, it is most useful where a modification of an agency decision is likely to satisfy the contesting parties. In many land use controversies, however, outright reversal or rejection of an agency decision is the only course of action that will satisfy affected citizens. Because it is unlikely that an agency will ever voluntarily agree to such a settlement, mediation will probably fail under these circumstances, no matter how skillful the mediators.

A related approach also suggested as a source of redress for administrative nonresponsiveness is the appointment of an ombudsman or citizen advocate. The ombudsman concept, as originally developed in Sweden, is that of a strong independent investigator

---

53. See Jane McCarthy, "Mediation: A New Approach to Environmental Disputes," unpublished manuscript, Office of Environmental Mediation, University of Washington, 1975.

who may intervene for the affected citizen when redress cannot be gained through ordinary political and legal channels.[54]

In the United States, the ombudsman approach has recently been implemented in several cities, but citizen advocates have typically been appointed *within* administrative agencies rather than as powerful autonomous investigators. Similarly, the idea of an independent consumer protection agency at the federal level has been abandoned and consumer advocates have recently been appointed within each agency instead. There is understandable skepticism among many citizen groups about whether such an internal ombudsman constitutes much of a significant advance in the public testing of administrative decisions. Without a guarantee of independence and autonomy, the internal ombudsman may easily be compromised.

The attraction of the ombudsman role, assuming that independent, impartial investigatory offices could be established in American jurisdictions, is that it could fulfill many of the same functions as judicial review of administrative actions without the cost, clumsiness, or extended adversary proceedings of litigation. The idea thus deserves further examination and experimentation.

A final approach to public testing, currently under extensive examination, derives from the old long-ballot movement. This involves subjecting top executives of administrative agencies and members of citizen regulatory commissions to some type of popular selection, thus allowing the general pattern of administrative actions to be reviewed and guided by the public. One election-like scheme for administrative appointments has been suggested by the Citizen's League of Minneapolis-St. Paul. In this approach, the public would not formally vote for members of decision-making boards, but would enjoy periodic opportunities to interrogate and evaluate administrative officials. As the League points out:

Opportunity for public evaluation is compelling because of the important decisions and recommendations these bodies make and the overall lack of public accountability for the selection of persons by multimember bodies.[55]

---

54. On the general concept of the ombudsman or citizen's advocate, see the collection of articles in Stanley V. Anderson, ed., *Ombudsman for American Government* (Englewood Cliffs, N.J.: Prentice Hall, 1968). See also Walter Gellhorn, *Ombudsman and Others: Citizen's Protectors in Nine Countries* (Cambridge, Mass.: Harvard University Press, 1966). The practical experience of ombudsmen in American cities is analyzed in "The Ombudsman: The Citizen's Advocate," *Management Information Service*, October 1969.

55. *An Election-Like Process for Appointments*, A Citizen's League Report (Minneapolis, Minn: The Citizen's League, April 1975), p. 26.

These evaluations would be used by the legislature and elected executives in making administrative appointments.

The primary problem with any type of election or quasielectoral procedure is that voter turnout and voter information levels are already so low in races for traditional elective offices that the prospects for intelligent issue-oriented participation in choosing administrative officials seem very slim. As with the original long-ballot movement, the consequence might well be the "capture" of administrative agencies by small, highly organized interest groups rather than an increase in the openness and responsiveness of such agencies. However, as Richard Stewart notes,

A more hopeful prognosis is possible. Elections might direct public attention to the fact of agency responsibility for major policy decisions. . . . Such developments could bring in their train more informed public scrutiny and control over agency policies, either through the electoral process or alternatives that might develop out of it.[56]

As yet, these rival hypotheses have not been adequately tested.

---

56. Richard Stewart, "The Reformation of American Administrative Law," 88 *Harvard Law Review* 1669, 1793 (1975).

VI. CONCLUSION: BENEFITS AND COSTS OF CITIZEN INVOLVEMENT

BENEFITS

After all the educational and informational materials have been distributed, the opinions collected and cataloged, the decisions made, explained, and tested, what is the long-term payoff of citizen involvement? What are the tangible benefits that may be expected from a program that is "effective" and "meaningful?"

The major benefits of an effective citizen involvement program are two: increasing the *civility* of the decision-making process and enhancing the *rationality* of policy decisions.

One of the most obvious symptoms of citizen discontent with the growth of administrative power is the breakdown in the civility of the decision-making process. Administrative decisions have become extraordinarily contentious and controversial. Far from the cool and dispassionate translation of policy into practice, administrative decision making has become the focus of much of the citizen militance and mobilization that has arisen in the past several decades. Emotional accusations of deference to vested interests, vilification of decision makers' motives, and charges of corruption and conspiracy have all become common characteristics of citizen opposition to administrative actions. In turn, decision makers often have reciprocated with hostile and defensive behavior of their own.

Underlying the degeneration of civility is a breakdown in the citizen's fundamental trust in government and belief that decision makers can be counted on to be fair and impartial in reaching decisions. This trust is essential to the efficient and purposeful functioning of government, for if a large proportion of decisions is contested, citizens can soon exhaust government and little can be accomplished.

Many decisions, even though they may be personally disagreeable to a substantial number of citizens, must nevertheless be accepted. This is not to advocate a deferential attitude toward government, based on idealized public relations imagery or uncritical patriotism. Rather, trust and civility must ultimately rest on citizen satisfaction with the openness, accessibility, and fairness of administrative decision making. As a program of citizen involvement improves these qualities, the benefits should be evident in better relations between citizens and decision makers and a decline in bitter, devisive struggles.

The second major benefit of an effective citizen involvement program is improving the rationality of governmental decisions. A rational decision is one based on an explicit calculus between the ends desired by a majority or plurality of citizens and the means available to government to achieve those ends. While American theories of public administration have traditionally relied on the concept of rational, objective decision making, it has become increasingly evident just how irrational and subjective many administrative decisions are.

As evidenced by citizen discontent and protest, the administrator's conception of the "public interest" is often based more on personal ideological convictions and biases than on a clear understanding of public desires and preferences. In addition, as innumerable legal reversals of arbitrary and capricious administrative decisions have demonstrated, the means-ends calculus between stated goals and adopted policies is often faulty.

An effective citizen involvement program contributes to more rational decisions by revealing the pattern of public preferences and by stimulating decision makers to incorporate this information explicitly in their deliberations and decisions. Of course, none of the citizen participation opportunities and requirements guarantees that administrative decision makers will respect public preferences in their policy decisions. This is why effective strategies are needed to test decisions through the courts, referenda, and other means. However, to the extent that involvement programs bring public preferences into the open and require administrative decision makers to explain and justify their decisions, citizen involvement should encourage more rational policy decisions—to the ultimate benefit of both citizens and decision makers.

Rational decision making, it must be stressed, neither requires nor implies rote responsiveness to majority or plurality preferences. There may be numerous occasions when those preferences should be overruled in a particular jurisdiction because of legal or technical considerations. For example, a neighborhood cannot necessarily expect to exclude a low-income housing project because a majority of neighborhood residents oppose it. Residents of a municipality cannot necessarily expect to deny a site for a proposed sewer plant because a majority or plurality of citizens oppose it.

Citizen involvement is not a substitute for sacrifice, nor an excuse for parochialism. The point is, however, that as a result of an effective citizen involvement program, the calculus that leads to a particular policy decision will be open and explicit. Citizen preferences will be clearly revealed, the reasons for acceptance or nonacceptance of citizen preferences spelled out, and the calculus tested in court or some other forum. Thus, the rationality of the decision is perfected and demonstrated.

Beyond the major benefits of citizen involvement, there are several possible subsidiary advantages. Perhaps the most important of these is the psychic reward to citizens that results from their involvement in decision making. While the evidence is scanty, political scientists and sociologists have found that many citizens markedly increase their sense of both self-esteem and personal political efficacy as a result of participating in a citizen involvement program.[1]

In addition, the community as a whole may benefit from a citizen involvement program as participation infuses voluntary organizations with greater vitality. This has happened, for example, in several cities that have used neighborhood organizations as key elements of citizen involvement programs. These organizations have subsequently expanded their memberships and functions beyond levels deemed feasible before the involvement program.

COSTS

Citizen involvement programs involve substantial amounts of time and money. However, these costs often have been exaggerated and magnified in legislative debates and public administration literature, and a straightforward analysis is urgently needed.

Let us first examine the cost in time. The fear of delay and paralysis of decision making crops up repeatedly as a central theme in discussions about citizen involvement. In reality, most aspects of citizen involvement require little more time to implement than would be expended in the course of the routine decision-making process. For instance, comprehensive land use planning requires the collection and processing of detailed information on a community, regardless of whether a program of citizen involvement is being implemented simultaneously. Similarly, administrative decisions on zoning and subdivision approvals still require thirty to sixty days advance notice and a formal public hearing, regardless of whether special public

---

1. See Richard Cole, *Citizen Participation and the Urban Policy Process* (Lexington, Mass.: Heath, 1974); Willis Sutton Jr., "Differential Perceptions of Impact of a Rural Anti-Poverty Campaign," 50 *Social Science Quarterly,* 657–667 (1969), and Robert Yin and Douglas Yates, *Street-Level Governments: Assessing Decentralization and Urban Services* (Washington, D.C., Rand Corporation, 1974).

preparation and participation efforts are being carried out during the same time.

Certainly, the public preparation and citizen participation components can be dragged out and can delay decisions in circumstances in which administrators strive for community consensus, or when special efforts to reach inactive segments of the community are involved. But the probable delays resulting from such efforts can be confronted directly during the design of the involvement program.

The costs of a particular program option can be calculated and an explicit decision can be made on whether the extra time is worthwhile. The point here is that the time involved in public preparation and citizen participation activity is not intrinsically unlimited and uncontrollable. Rather, the time allotted to a structured sequence of citizen involvement activities can be specified before the program is implemented.

Protracted delay and impairment of administrative efficiency most often arise in the governmental accountability phase of a citizen involvement program. Of greatest concern are the seemingly endless delays of administrative action resulting from litigation. In many instances, legal proceedings have consumed three to four years. However, one may question whether these costs are an intrinsic fault of citizen involvement. Is the congestion of the American civil courts a problem of citizen involvement or a failure of judicial management?

It is true that recent statutes have greatly liberalized standing requirements and have added to the caseload of the civil courts. Some critics imply that most cases brought by newly authorized parties are frivolous and do not really deserve their day in court to test the fairness and responsiveness of administrative decisions. However, based on the record of reversals and remands won by public interest groups and citizen organizations under the new access rules, this implication clearly is not valid. Thus, the appropriate solution to delay may lie in authorizing more judges or requiring judges to handle their cases more expeditiously rather than in limiting severely the availability of judicial review.

This is not to deny that some citizen groups use delay for delay's sake, pyramiding court challenges in the hope that government can ultimately be exhausted. As emphasized in Chapter V, access to the courts must be carefully considered in the context of the overall citizen involvement program, including other available or appropriate means of testing administrative decisions. However, concern about delays should not be used as an excuse for drastically limiting the role of litigation in citizen involvement.

With regard to other means of insuring accountability, there are no insurmountable barriers to expeditious decision making. Legislatures can enact special rules for referenda to decrease the time lag. An ombudsman can be required to operate within a structured timetable of procedural review. Mediation experts can be given a specific deadline for concluding their work.

In sum, the intrinsic time costs of citizen involvement in administrative decision making appear considerably lower than many critics have contended. There is no denying that the cumulative time requirements of a citizen involvement program may impose some delay in decision making. Yet, why should basic improvements in the civility and rationality of decision making be sacrificed for the sake of marginal advantages in "administrative efficiency?" Obviously there is some point at which time costs become excessive and the efficiency of decision making becomes an overriding consideration. However, delays do not seem inherently unmanageable and appropriate attention to the design of a citizen involvement program can keep time costs under firm control.

With regard to the monetary costs of citizen involvement, it should first be emphasized that many aspects of an involvement program may be subsumed under the normal and necessary expenditures of administrative decision making. Urban planners may take calls from citizens or conduct meetings without significant impact on their other work. Referenda can be held during regularly scheduled elections without much extra expense. Courts function whether or not they ever take a land use case. Hearing notices and decision documents are typically printed in substantial quantity even if they are never systematically distributed to citizens. Under all these circumstances, the funds would be expended anyway, even if a citizen involvement program did not tap available resources for its own purposes. Indeed, most citizen involvement programs are conducted primarily through such indirect expenditures.

The bulk of the direct expense of a citizen involvement program arises in preparing and distributing educational and informational materials. Such costs include special personnel or consultants to prepare these materials, postage and printing expenses, and extra clerical help. To some extent, the cost of information dissemination can be controlled by exploiting existing resources in the community. Free media coverage can be sought, the public schools and adult education courses can be used for basic education on land use, colleges and universities can often be tapped for assistance in preparing materials, and citizen organizations can be used for free dissemination. Nevertheless, the bulk of the education and information cost must typically be borne directly if the involvement program is to reach a substantial proportion of affected citizens.

Direct costs will vary substantially, depending on how far the program attempts to reach out to inactive citizens and which specific techniques are utilized. However, baseline costs can be specified.[2] In an intensive planning, policy-definition, or rule-making effort, the direct cost of effective public preparation is likely to run between seventy cents and one dollar per household per year. This assumes that the citizen involvement program takes advantage of free community resources. Thus, for example, in a city of 100,000 population with 30,000 households, the public preparation component of citizen involvement in comprehensive planning would cost between $20,000 and $30,000.

In a less intensive setting of decision making, such as granting permits, approving subdivisions, or zoning, education and information dissemination is more sporadic and thus less expensive. A reasonable baseline cost here is between thirty and fifty cents per household per year, resulting in an expenditure of between $10,000 and $15,000 for the sample community just cited.

The citizen participation component of an involvement program relies primarily on meetings, forums, task forces, and hearings. These techniques, as well as supplementary methods of review and comment by mail or telephone, typically involve only small direct costs—some extra staff time, rental of meeting space, duplicating expenses, and postage. All these techniques rely basically on the volunteer efforts of citizens and decision makers.

Substantial direct costs can be incurred in the use of surveys or high-technology approaches such as two-way cable television and teaching computers. Surveys, for example, can cost from ten to fifteen dollars per respondent for a brief questionnaire conducted by professional consultants. With a typical sample size of 1,000 in a fair-sized community, a single survey may cost as much as all the public education and information activities combined.

Similarly, the initial capital cost of setting up a large electronic communications link such as the Televote system in San Jose, California, may well be more than $100,000. However, as emphasized

---

2. These estimates are derived from comparative analysis of the costs incurred in six citizen involvement programs. The evaluation of these programs is reported in Nelson Rosenbaum, *State Land Use Controls: An Evaluation of Citizen Involvement in Decision Making* (Washington, D.C., The Urban Institute, forthcoming).

In the preceding chapter, these more costly techniques are clearly supplementary to the basic methods of citizen participation. For example, a major sample survey may only be necessary and appropriate once in the course of a multiyear planning program and may be used even less frequently in the course of regulatory decision making.

In the final phase of a citizen involvement program—governmental accountability—significant direct costs may be incurred in establishing an ombudsman's or advocate's office. In a jurisdiction of 100,000 people, such an office might cost $40,000 to $60,000 per year. However, most jurisdictions would need such services in land use disputes only a small fraction of the time. Complaints about land use decisions of administrative agencies could typically be handled by a general ombudsmen's office in a state or municipality as part of its overall caseload. Mediators would be needed on a part-time consultant basis only in the most serious and controversial disputes. Thus, even if a community does supplement the basic techniques of referenda, litigation, and elections with these new approaches, direct costs are likely to be quite small in relation to the overall expenditure for administrative decision making.

In summary, the costs of citizen involvement are manageable and controllable, not by crude budgetary limitations but by careful investigation and specification of the time and monetary expenditures required to carry out each aspect of a program. If a program skillfully exploits available resources in government and the community, direct expenditures can be quite limited in relation to the overall cost of administrative decision making. Of course, some jurisdictions may not be able to afford even small expenditures on citizen involvement. However, this handicap is no excuse for avoiding the issue with overblown rhetoric about the excessive delays and unmanageable expenditures generated by citizen involvement programs.

NEED FOR EVALUATION AND OVERSIGHT

Legislatures and elected executives have chosen to delegate broad discretionary authority to administrative agencies in the field of land use. They have also chosen to counterbalance those grants of discretion by authorizing systematic citizen involvement in the decision-making process. Those who write such mandates have a basic responsibility to insure that citizen involvement is more than an empty slogan. This responsibility includes not only more active supervision of the design and implementation of citizen involvement programs, but also periodic oversight and evaluation of program results. Have the funds and time allocated been sufficient to put together a coherent effective program? Has the program enhanced citizen trust and the civility of administrative decision making? Do administrative decisions seem more objective and rational as a consequence of the citizen involvement program? What improvements in procedure and technique are required? Only the legislature and elected executive, with the assistance of citizen participants, can definitively answer these questions.

These issues are perhaps best illustrated in the approach to citizen involvement established by the land use law (S.B. 100) Oregon enacted in 1973. The Oregon statute is quite explicit about the importance attached to citizen involvement in municipal decision-making processes and specifies a number of minimum design features to be incorporated in involvement programs. To insure that legislative intent is respected and to provide more extensive guidance to local agencies, S.B. 100 also established a State Citizen Involvement Advisory Committee composed of twenty appointed citizens. The committee has developed a set of explicit citizen involvement goals and guidelines for local land use planning and regulatory agencies. It also exercises direct review and oversight responsibility for the design of citizen involvement programs proposed by these jurisdictions.

Each local legislature submitting a proposed citizen involvement plan is required to spell out the rationale for its design decisions and to justify the expenditure level for the involvement program. Each legislature also is required to submit a periodic evaluation of its involvement program, based on assessment criteria specified in the state goals and guidelines.

This elaborate procedure has aroused considerable opposition among Oregon's smaller cities and towns, but it does illustrate a serious and active role for legislatures and elected executives in the implementation of citizen involvement. If such involvement is to be firmly established as an effective antidote to growing administrative power and as a normal, necessary aspect of American democratic practice, legislators and elected executives must accept this responsibility in a positive and committed way.

FURTHER READINGS

The readings listed below are provided as a practical reference guide to the literature on citizen involvement. Sources are cited under five general headings, corresponding to the major chapters of the text.

CITIZEN INVOLVEMENT AND DEMOCRATIC PRACTICE

Peter Bachrach, *The Theory of Democratic Elitism* (Boston: Little Brown, 1967).

Daniel Kramer, *Participatory Democracy: Developing Ideals of the Political Left* (Cambridge, Mass.: Schenkman Publishing Co., 1972).

Melvin Mogulof, *Citizen Participation: A Review and Commentary on Federal Policies and Practices* (Washington, D.C. The Urban Institute, 1970).

Sidney Verba, "Democratic Participation," *The Annals of the American Academy of Political and Social Science,* No. 373, September 1967, pp. 53–78.

David Ricci, *Community Power and Democratic Theory* (New York: Random House, 1971).

Emmett Redford, *Democracy in the Administrative State* (New York: Oxford University Press, 1969).

Herbert Kaufman, "Administrative Decentralization and Political Power," *Public Administration Review,* 29(1969), pp. 3–14.

Carl Stenberg, "Citizens and the Administrative State: From Participation to Power," *Public Administration Review,* 32(1972), pp. 190–198.

Richard Stewart, "The Reformation of American Administrative Law," 88 *Harvard Law Review* 1669(1975).

James C. Cunningham, "Citizen Participation in Public Affairs," *Public Administration Review,* 32(1972), pp. 589–602.

STRUCTURE OF CITIZEN INVOLVEMENT PROGRAMS

John C. Hendee et. al., *Public Involvement and the Forest Service* (Washington, D.C.: U.S. Forest Service, 1973).

Desmond Connor, *Citizens Participate: An Action Guide for Public Issues* (Oakville, Ontario: Development Press, 1974).

G. A. Ayer, *Guidelines for Public Participation in the Transportation Planning Process* (Downsview, Ontario: Ministry of Transportation and Communications, Ontario; 1972).

Howard S. Sargent Jr., "Fishbowl Planning Immerses Pacific Northwest Citizens in Corps Projects," *Civil Engineering,* 42(1972), pp. 54–57.

Committee on Public Participation in Planning (Skeffington Committee) *People and Planning* (London: H.M.S.O., 1969).

Melvin Mogulof, *Citizen Participation: The Local Perspective* (Washington, D.C.: The Urban Institute, 1970).

Sherry Arnstein, "A Ladder of Citizen Participation," *American Institute of Planners Journal,* 35(1969), pp. 216–224.

A. Bruce Bishop, *Public Participation in Water Resource Planning* (Arlington, Va.: U.S. Army Engineer Institute of Water Resources, 1970).

Ernest Gellhorn, "Public Participation in Administrative Proceedings," *Yale Law Journal* 81(1972), pp. 359–404.

Marvin Manheim et. al., *Community Values in Highway Location and Design: A Procedural Guide* (Cambridge, Mass.: M.I.T., 1971).

ISSUES OF PROGRAM DESIGN

Alan Altshuler, *Community Control* (New York: Pegasus, 1970).

Gilbert Herbert, "The Neighborhood Unit Principle and Organic Theory," *Sociological Review,* 11(1963), pp. 165–213.

James Q. Wilson, "Planning and Politics: Citizen Participation in Urban Renewal," *Journal of the American Institute of Planners* 29(1963), pp. 242–249.

Hans B. C. Spiegel and Stephen Mittenthal, *Neighborhood Power and Control: Implications for Urban Planning* (New York: Columbia University, Institute for Urban Environment, 1968).

Adam Herbert, "Management Under Conditions of Decentralization and Citizen Participation," *Public Administration Review,* 32(1972), pp. 622–637.

Charles V. Hamilton, "Racial Ethnic, and Social Class Politics and Administration," *Public Administration Review,* 32(1972), pp. 638–648.

Roger Jowell, *A Review of Public Involvement in Planning* (London: Social and Community Planning Research, 1976).

Susan Fainstein and Norman Fainstein, "Local Control as Social Reform: Planning for Big Cities in the Seventies," *Journal of the American Institute of Planners,* 42(1976), pp. 175–285.

Stephen Cupps, "Emerging Issues of Citizen Participation," Paper presented to 1975 National Conference, American Society for Public Administration, Chicago, Ill.: April, 1975.

Daniel P. Moynihan, *Maximum Feasible Misunderstanding: Community Action in the War on Poverty* (New York: Free Press, 1969).

METHODS OF PROGRAM IMPLEMENTATION

William B. Shore, *Listening to the Metropolis: Handbook on Public Participation in Regional Planning* (New York: Regional Plan Association, 1974).

Jerome Saroff, *The Use of Opinion Surveys and Sampling Techniques in the Planning Process* (Anchorage, Alaska: Development Research Associates, Inc., 1969).

Lisa Peattie, "Reflections on Advocacy Planning," *Journal of the American Institute of Planners* 34(1968), pp. 80–88.

Walter Gellhorn, *Ombudsmen and Others: Citizen's Protectors in Wine Countries* (Cambridge, Mass.: Harvard University Press, 1966).

Amitai Etzioni et. al., "Minerva: A Participatory Technology System," *Bulletin of the Atomic Scientists,* 27(1971), pp. 4–12.

Joseph Sax, *Defending the Environment: A Strategy for Citizen Action* (New York: Knopf, 1971).

Jane McCarthy, "Mediation: A New Approach to Environmental Disputes," Institute for Environmental Studies, University of Washington, September, 1975.

Ellis Walton and Jerome Saroff, "Proposed Strategy for Public Hearings," *Highway Research Board,* 356(1971), pp. 26–32.

Thomas Borton, Katharine Warner, and J. William Wenrich, *The Susquehanna Communication-Participation Study: Selected Approaches to Public Involvement in Water Resources Planning* (Arlington, Va.: U.S. Army Engineer Institute of Water Resources, 1970).

Jay Wollenberg et. al., "Capacity-Building: An Alternative Approach to

Citizen Involvement in Planning,'' Department of Urban and Regional Studies, Massachusetts Institute of Technology, March 1975.

COSTS AND BENEFITS OF CITIZEN INVOLVEMENT

Robert Aleshire, ''Planning and Citizen Participation: Costs, Benefits, and Approaches,'' *Urban Affairs Quarterly,* (1970), pp. 369–393.

Norman Wengert, ''Public Participation in Water Planning: A Critique of Theory, Doctrine, and Practice,'' *Water Resources Bulletin,* 7(1971), pp. 26–32.

Walter Rosenbaum, ''Slaying Beautiful Hypotheses With Ugly Facts: EPA and the Limits of Public Participation,'' Paper presented to the 1975 National Conference, American Society of Public Administration, Chicago, Ill.: May 1975.

Daniel Mazmanian, ''Citizens and the Assessment of Technology: An Examination of the Participation Thesis,'' Paper delivered to the 1974 Annual Meeting of the American Political Science Association, Chicago, Illinois, September 1974.

Harlan Cleveland, ''How Do You Get Everybody In On the Act and Still Get Some Action,'' *Public Management* 57(1975), pp. 3–6.

Nelson M. Rosenbaum, *State Land Use Controls: An Evaluation of Citizen Involvement in Decision-Making* (Washington, D.C.: The Urban Institute, forthcoming).

Judy Rosener, *The CALTRANS Public Participation Program: An Evaluation and Recommendations* (Irvine, Cal.: U.C. Irvine, Graduate School of Public Administration, September, 1975).

Richard Cole, *Citizen Participation and the Urban Policy Process* (Lexington, Mass.: Lexington Books, 1974).

Booz, Allen, and Hamilton Public Administration Services, *Citizen Participation in the Model Cities Program* (Washington, D.C.: Department of Housing and Urban Development, 1971).

Anthony Downs, ''Citizen Participation in Community Development: Why Some Changes Are Needed,'' *National Civic Review,* 64(1975), pp. 238–248.